VASE OF POMPEII

Lajos Walder c. 1943

Also by Lajos Walder

Tyrtaeus: A Tragedy
Below Zero: A Play
The Complete Plays

Lajos Walder

VASE OF POMPEII
A Play

*Translated from the Hungarian
by Agnes Walder*

Upper West Side Philosophers, Inc.
New York

Upper West Side Philosophers, Inc. provides a publication venue for original philosophical thinking steeped in lived life, in line with our motto: *philosophical living & lived philosophy.*

Published by Upper West Side Philosophers, Inc. / P. O. Box 250645, New York, NY 10025, USA

www.westside-philosophers.com / www.yogaforthemind.us

Originally published as *Pompeji Váza* in *Pompeji* (Budapest: Maecenas, 1990)

Copyright © 2016 The Children of the late Dr Lajos Walder
English Translation Copyright © 2016 Agnes Walder
Translator's Preface & Afterword Copyright © 2016 Agnes Walder

All rights reserved. No part of this publication may be reproduced, stored in a retrieval system, or transmitted, in any form or by any means, electronic, mechanical, photocopying, recording, or otherwise, without prior permission in writing from the publisher. For all inquiries concerning permission to reuse material from any of our titles, contact the publisher in writing, or the Copyright Clearance Center, Inc. (CCC), 222 Rosewood Drive, Danvers, MA 01923, USA (www.copyright.com).

Cover art based on "Die Bucht von Neapel," C. H. Kniep, 1787.

The colophon is a registered trademark
of Upper West Side Philosophers, Inc.

Library of Congress Cataloging-in-Publication Data

Names: Walder, Lajos, 1913-1945, author. | Walder, Agnes, translator.
Title: Vase of Pompeii : a play / Lajos Walder ; translated from the Hungarian by Agnes Walder.
Other titles: Pompeji Vaza. English
Description: New York : Upper West Side Philosophers, Inc., 2017.
Identifiers: LCCN 2016033486 (print) | LCCN 2016043358 (ebook) | ISBN 9781935830375 (pbk.) | ISBN 9781935830405 ()
Subjects: LCSH: Walder, Lajos, 1913-1945--Translations into English.
Classification: LCC PH3351.W35 P613 2017 (print) | LCC PH3351.W35 (ebook) |
DDC 894.511232--dc23
LC record available at https://lccn.loc.gov/2016033486

Designed by UWSP
Printed in the United States of America

CONTENTS

Translator's Preface / 7
Vase of Pompeii / 11
Translator's Afterword / 73

From your children to your children's children

.

"That's why poets so often resort to writing plays."
—Joseph Brodsky

TRANSLATOR'S PREFACE

"You must try to work always, under any circumstances."
Dmitri Shostakovich

Lajos Walder (1913-1945), my father—poet, playwright and attorney-at-law, whose Hungarian pseudonym was 'Vándor' ('Wanderer')—was well known as a poet in Budapest in the 1930s; yet he was never known as a playwright. He wrote his plays in the harshest of circumstances and in secret in the early 1940s while intermittently serving in a Jewish forced labor battalion. He wrote them without the slightest chance of having them staged or printed, since by then the works of Jewish artists could, by law, no longer be performed or published in Hungary. Today, we are left with the wistful thought that, in those terrible times, he may have at least lived with the hope that one day his plays might find a home in print and on stage. Indeed, throughout the years of organizing and translating my father's plays, this thought has been my abiding inspiration.

Not only were my father's plays completely unknown in his native Hungary, but even as manuscripts they had no physical presence in that country for twenty-eight years. In 1961, my grandmother Ida Walder brought out my father's unpublished manuscripts to our family, who had emigrated to Sydney, Australia, in 1957. In 1989, I returned to Hungary for the launch of the posthumous publication of a volume of my father's selected poems, entitled *A Poet Lived Here Amongst You*. At that time, I took with me copies of the plays in order to show them to the late Géza Hegedüs, renowned literary critic and professor of drama at the University of Budapest. A year later, in 1990, two of my father's three extant plays, *Tyrtaeus* and *Vase of Pompeii*, were published in their original Hungarian under the title *Pompeji*. His third play, *Below Zero*, was planned for a later publication in Hungary.

In his foreword to *Pompeji*, Géza Hegedüs wrote: "In aesthetic value and nuance, the plays differ from the grotesque tartness of Walder's tragi-comic poems, but they are comparable to them in being the uniquely beautiful creations of an original mind." (My father's complete poems in English were published by Upper West Side Philosophers, Inc. in 2015, under the title *Become a Message: Poems*. That volume also contains a detailed synopsis of my father's brief life, which tragically ended on the day of his liberation from the Gunskirchen concentration camp on May 4, 1945.)

In the early post-war years in Hungary, my mother tried repeatedly to have my father's plays staged. She knew several directors and actors personally—many of them from my father's erstwhile literary circle. One particularly close friend of my father's was a highly gifted actor and director. Season after season, he promised my mother that he would see to it that the plays—starting with *Tyrtaeus*—were performed, but this never eventuated. Finally, when my mother tried to pin him down on a firm date, he said that he would have Tyrtaeus put on, on the condition that he himself be named as the playwright. Following this betrayal, my mother did not try to bring attention to the plays again, especially once communist censorship was in place, which made the eventual success of her endeavors highly unlikely.

We don't know the order in which the plays were written. My beloved mother, died in Sydney in 1973. In my conversations with her about my father's work, the sequence in which the plays had been created somehow never came up. My uncle Imre Walder (the other person closest to my father and his literary legacy) was not present when my father composed the plays. The labor battalion my uncle had been assigned to was sent to the Russian front in early 1942, and by the time he returned to Hungary from Russian captivity, my father was no longer alive. Incidentally, the typewritten original of *Vase of Pompeii* bears a copyright stamp in Hungarian and in French. The date on the stamp is February 10, 1944. Nazi Germany invaded Hungary on 19 March 1944. Plans for the annihilation of the Hungarian Jews were already in place by then.

Translator's Preface

My father was a certified attorney, who had completed his articles just prior to the official institution of the Jewish laws, which barred Jews from practicing in the professions. Indeed, he made ample use of his knowledge of the law in all three of his plays.

From 1942 onward, we only have a handful of poems from my father. With the future so highly uncertain, and forced labor increasingly robbing him of time, he must have made the decision to give the plays priority. Under the circumstances, he was probably looking for a broader expression of his philosophical beliefs than poetry would have allowed him. He had been familiar with the works of Aldous Huxley, Louis Aragon and Louis-Ferdinand Céline, who had begun as poets and continued in prose; he loved the theater and was influenced by Oscar Wilde and the progressive George Bernard Shaw, as well as by German and French playwrights, such as Victorien Sardou; he was equally aware of the works of the Austrian poet and playwright Hugo von Hofmannsthal and the Belgian dramatist Maurice Maeterlinck. Given the strong emphasis on Greek and Latin education in prewar Hungary, moreover, my father was widely conversant with classical Greek and Roman authors as well as the French classics, especially with the works of Jean Racine. His plays are densely packed with insights so pertinent that they seem universally valid even today.

His "was the most credible voice to express the times between the two world wars," Géza Hegedüs has written about my father's poetry. The same holds true for his plays, and in particular for *Tyrtaeus*. Now—well over seventy years after they were written—*Tyrtaeus*, *Vase of Pompeii*, and *Below Zero* are brand-new plays for the English stage.

In the long battle for recognition of my father's remarkable literary talent, I have often thought of Max Brod. Our stories are not at all parallel. But if Max Brod had heeded the wish of his best friend, Franz Kafka, to have all of his works destroyed after his death, world literature would be that much poorer. Similar thoughts have driven me regarding my father's legacy.

VASE OF POMPEII

CAST

MONSIEUR ROBERT LEBORDIN, retired Director of the Institute of Antiquities / Art Collector / Uncle Gustave the pawnbroker

ROBBIE, Lebordin at fifteen

BOB, Lebordin at twenty

ROBERT, Lebordin at thirty

MONSIEUR ROBERT, Lebordin at forty

ANGELA, the visitor / Angela the kept woman / Angela the arist's model / Angie the prostitute / Angela the American millionairess.

MONSIEUR LATOUR, Monsieur Robert's father-in-law

The action takes place in the one-room apartment of Monsieur Robert Lebordin in Paris in the early 1930s.

ACT I

The curtain rises to reveal a one-room apartment. Stage left contains a kitchenette that is separated from the main part of the stage by a dividing wall with an access door in the center. On the back wall, towards stage left, is a door leading to the hallway. Towards stage right there is a door that leads onto the balcony overlooking a courtyard. Center-stage, towards stage right, is a door that leads into the bathroom. Stage right is otherwise overcrowded with furniture. On the shelves are books, pictures, vases, statues: things of serious value, all jumbled together. On top of a low cupboard, there is a large picture leaning back to front against the wall. A bottle of whisky and two glasses are in the cupboard, out of sight. Downstage towards stage right, in a prominent place on one of the shelves sits the Vase of Pompeii. The vase should be an Arretine molded form of unpainted pottery. The human figures on it should appear to have been carved. Center-stage are a desk and a chair. There are a jug of water, a glass, writing implements and a telephone on the desk. Downstage center are two armchairs with a coffee table between them.

Monsieur Lebordin is in the kitchenette preparing to heat some milk on the stove. He is a tall balding man who looks older than his sixty years. As he lights the gas under the pot, he momentarily staggers. He tries to recover, but is overtaken by another more severe attack. He panics and stumbles, crashing into some pots or utensils that fall from the counter. He makes for the left armchair downstage and collapses into it. He whimpers and goes into spasms as the attack increases in strength. At that moment, the milk boils over. A sharp ringing of the doorbell cuts through the air. Then, again and again, the doorbell keeps ringing. The curtain goes down for a few seconds. When it goes up again, the doorbell continues ringing, even more insistently. Slowly, as one who is waking up from a trance, Lebordin makes for the door. He goes into the hallway, leaving the door open behind him, and calls out through the window in the hallway.

Vase of Pompeii

MONSIEUR LEBORDIN: Yes. Who are you looking for?
ANGELA: (*Her voice from outside*) I am looking for Monsieur le Directeur, Robert Lebordin.
MONSIEUR LEBORDIN: Yes. What is it?
ANGELA: I would like to ask a favor of you.
MONSIEUR LEBORDIN: Oh, well, that's different. (*The key turns in the lock*) Come in, please. I'll lead the way if you don't mind. Only don't ask me for money. Today is the 27th, and I don't have any money left. I get my pension on the 30th. Until then, I would ask for your kind patience ... (*At this point they step into the room*)
ANGELA: (*A very beautiful, tall and stylish woman. She is wearing a loose, blouse-like, Grecian-style white silk dress with a broad gold belt at her waist. She is holding an enormous bouquet of crimson roses in her hand*) I am asking, Monsieur, but not for money.
MONSIEUR LEBORDIN: Spare me the riddles, mademoiselle, get to the point! I've had a rather difficult day. I feel dizzy and my heart is playing up ...
ANGELA: With your good reputation, the heart must be flawless.
MONSIEUR LEBORDIN: I'll take that as a compliment, mademoiselle. (*He notices that Angela is examining the room*) And might one inquire as to your name?
ANGELA: Angela.
MONSIEUR LEBORDIN: Not a surname, but a beautiful name.
ANGELA: Forgive me, it's not lack of trust, but I'll only give you my surname if you agree to my request.
MONSIEUR LEBORDIN: (*A little pause*) Please, sit down.
ANGELA: (*They sit. Embarrassed because of the roses in her hand*) The roses ... where could I ...
MONSIEUR LEBORDIN: Give them to me. I'll put them in the kitchen.
ANGELA: Isn't there a vase here somewhere?
MONSIEUR LEBORDIN: Of course there is. In fact I have several vases in this apartment. One of them is a relic of Pompeii. (*Pause*) But do you think it would be appropriate to put flowers

that will last for two days into a vase that has lasted for two thousand years?
ANGELA: (*A little indignantly*) But surely a vase exists for the purpose of ...
MONSIEUR LEBORDIN: No, mademoiselle. A vase is a vase and flowers are flowers. Did it ever occur to you to hang a funeral wreath onto a painting by Rembrandt? In this room there are several vases. But not one into which flowers could be put.
ANGELA: Well, I can take them back. (*She is standing embarrassed*)
MONSIEUR LEBORDIN: No, don't take them back, because there is no way you could put them back.
ANGELA: I thought you liked ...
MONSIEUR LEBORDIN: ... I like flowers. In their place. All things, I like in their place.
ANGELA: (*Laughing*) But it's so messy in here ...
MONSIEUR LEBORDIN: Yes, perhaps it would appear so. In your eyes, mademoiselle. Because your idea of order is to put dead flowers in a vase that has been alive for the last two thousand years. According to you, everything here is untidy because everything here is dusty. (*Angela nods*) You're mistaken, mademoiselle, because even the dust is in its proper place.
ANGELA: (*A little confidentially*) Yes ... yes ... They told me you were a strange person.
MONSIEUR LEBORDIN: If the truth be known, what's really strange is the commonplace tone you use when you talk about what's strange.
ANGELA: (*Almost crying*) Please, I'd rather go.
MONSIEUR LEBORDIN: If you'd rather go, then stay rather. (*He picks up the Vase of Pompeii from the shelf and places it on the coffee table*) Put the flowers in the vase. But do not think of adding water. The figures on the vase might think there was a flood. And now—tell me why you came.
ANGELA: I want to ask you for a recommendation.
MONSIEUR LEBORDIN: (*Sniggers a little sarcastically*) I was absolutely right. You see a little mess, and you talk of my disorder. Yet you think it entirely in order to ask for a reference from a

complete stranger. I can only be sincerely glad, mademoiselle, that in the world that you come from I am merely a pensioner.
ANGELA: Is that a refusal?
MONSIEUR LEBORDIN: I refuse your world but not your request. Then again, I can hardly do justice to your request. These days, I am just a retired Director.
ANGELA: But you have powerful friends. Even today, the undersecretary of state, Monsieur Lefevre ...
MONSIEUR LEBORDIN: ... is my friend. And I do not ask favors from my friends.
ANGELA: Professor Henri ...
MONSIEUR LEBORDIN: ... is my greatest professional nemesis. Because of the vases. He may not put flowers in the vases, but he manufactures theories about them. Bad theories. You know what, mademoiselle, you are right. One should rather put flowers in the vases than manufacture bad theories about them.
ANGELA: (*Stubbornly*) May I have a few lines of recommendation for Professor Henri.
MONSIEUR LEBORDIN: Mademoiselle, that is out of the question.
ANGELA: But it is very important.
MONSIEUR LEBORDIN: Dissertation?
ANGELA: No.
MONSIEUR LEBORDIN: Job?
ANGELA: No. Well, not exactly a job.
MONSIEUR LEBORDIN: This is positively hellish, mademoiselle. You, a total stranger, you walk in just like that and ask me to recommend you to my greatest adversary.
ANGELA: Please, I implore you!
MONSIEUR LEBORDIN: Then, again, maybe it's not that hellish after all. I will recommend you, mademoiselle. But first tell me, why did you come specifically to me? To such an old man?
ANGELA: It seemed the least dangerous.
MONSIEUR LEBORDIN: How so?
ANGELA: Well, how could I have gone to a young man? He

Act I

would've immediately misunderstood the situation. But about you I know ...

MONSIEUR LEBORDIN: You know nothing about me!

ANGELA: I know that you won't take advantage of the situation. If you were younger ... perhaps I'd have to give you something first ...

MONSIEUR LEBORDIN: You're right. If I were younger ... But I'm not—I'm old. Very well then. If I were younger I would be taking the flowers to you. This bunch of roses is truly symbolic of the chasm that's gaping between us. So now I thank you, I thank you for the flowers; which is rather an odd comment from me, since I doubt it is at all customary to give thanks for flowers that are brought to one's grave. Because it would be difficult to imagine a present that has a sadder significance for a living man. Anyway, tell me a bit about yourself. Who are you? What are you?

ANGELA: Just a girl.

MONSIEUR LEBORDIN: I see. And such a girl as yourself, will you get your man? Will it be success, or bankruptcy?

ANGELA: No, all I meant by this is that I'm still a girl. Therefore I can't tell you too much about myself. I would like to become an art historian, because art is eternal.

MONSIEUR LEBORDIN: A rather academic notion, mademoiselle. One day when you'll become a woman, you will realize that love is eternal. And that art is only history. The eternal history of love. And so, little girl, I know all there is to know about you and in my opinion you are no brighter than a senior associate of Professor Henri needs to be. I am therefore willing to ask him a favor, knowing that it will ultimately prove to be detrimental to him. He will surely be bewitched by your beauty, and he is, of course, younger than I am, and so he will no doubt conclude that you are as clever as you are beautiful. Tsk, tsk, poor Henri. How on earth could I recommend you? (*He gets up from the armchair and goes to the desk*) I'm being awful, am I not? Please, forgive me. I am sixty years old, and in sixty years I never had the opportunity to be awful to someone as beautiful as you. (*He sits down at the desk and starts to write. He writes a few lines. Angela is very much*

Vase of Pompeii

alarmed. Lebordin stands up pen in hand) There, please, read it.
ANGELA: (*Doesn't move*) Thank you very much.
MONSIEUR LEBORDIN: There is nothing to thank me for. Well, why don't you read it? Or do you want me to read it? (*Angela nods*) "Dear Henri! The bearer of these lines ..." Tsk, damn, I've referred to you only as Angela—naturally, since I still don't know your surname, oh well, it doesn't matter—so, "Dear Henri, Angela came to me for a few words of recommendation to you. As I am, in fact, doing this, you can see that I am not your enemy after all, because she clearly has no need of my praise. Your greatest adversary till death, Robert Lebordin." Mademoiselle ...
ANGELA: Monsieur le Directeur, perhaps you should also have added that I am aiming for the position of associate professor.
MONSIEUR LEBORDIN: Not necessary. You have managed to persuade me to write a letter to Henri. I have a feeling that from the moment you arrive, you will be the professor not the associate professor ...
ANGELA: You are a good person after all, Monsieur Lebordin.
MONSIEUR LEBORDIN: I'd like to believe it. Do you need me to see you out?
ANGELA: (*Jumps up, a little hurt at this quick dismissal*) No, thank you. (*There is a little pause, as if she were waiting to be held back. Lebordin suddenly grabs his chest*) Wouldn't it be better if I stay until somebody comes?
MONSIEUR LEBORDIN: Please, be good enough, a glass of water! Not for the flowers, for me. (*He drags himself to the armchair*)
ANGELA: (*Almost screaming*) Monsieur!
MONSIEUR LEBORDIN: The water, the water!
ANGELA: (*Pours water from the jug on the desk*) Here.
MONSIEUR LEBORDIN: (*Drinks*) Thank you, I feel better already.
ANGELA: See, what a little water can do?
MONSIEUR LEBORDIN: Not a little water—a little goodness.
ANGELA: Look, Monsieur Lebordin, I'll stay with you until somebody comes. I won't leave you alone in this condition.

Act I

MONSIEUR LEBORDIN: I live alone Angela—sooner or later you will have to leave.

ANGELA: I don't have to (*She tears up the letter of recommendation*) At worst, I won't become an associate professor. Art is not only an academic subject.

MONSIEUR LEBORDIN: I always felt it to be so. Art is not only an academic subject. The quality of goodness is also an art. There is no greater art than a little goodness. The art of the good. And by the way, art that contains no goodness cannot be true art. What a god-given great artist one has to be to be good in today's world, where ammunition factories are used to solve the problem of unemployment. Do you know why people are so bad? Because they are bunglers, and they love kitsch. Kitsch-loving bunglers. The League of Nations, orphanages. Orphanages, created by ammunition factories. And they scramble to buy more ammunition shares so that they can support more orphanages.

ANGELA: You speak the truth, Monsieur Lebordin. Only you tell your truth a little strangely.

MONSIEUR LEBORDIN: A truth that can be stated simply is not interesting enough to interest us.

ANGELA: (*Simply*) Is there anything I can do for you?

MONSIEUR LEBORDIN: Oh that's charming. You come here for my patronage, and now I've become your protégé. Tell me something comforting. I don't at all mind that you are not very clever. If you were, perhaps you wouldn't be so good, so kind.

ANGELA: How do you know that I am good, that I'm kind?

MONSIEUR LEBORDIN: I can feel it.

ANGELA: And do you believe in feelings?

MONSIEUR LEBORDIN: I do.

ANGELA: Then why do you speak so strangely. As if you were disillusioned with everything.

MONSIEUR LEBORDIN: I am disillusioned with everything.

ANGELA: How is it possible that you believe in feelings and yet you are disillusioned with everything?

MONSIEUR LEBORDIN: I cannot answer that now.

ANGELA: Would you like a wet towel on your forehead?

Vase of Pompeii

MONSIEUR LEBORDIN: Thank you, no.

ANGELA: You are a bad patient.

MONSIEUR LEBORDIN: And you would make a good nurse.

ANGELA: What makes you think that?

MONSIEUR LEBORDIN: Because it doesn't disillusion you that I believe in feelings yet I am disillusioned with everything.

ANGELA: Don't you want to lie down for a bit?

MONSIEUR LEBORDIN: I'm not sleepy.

ANGELA: But you don't feel well.

MONSIEUR LEBORDIN: No, I don't feel unwell. I would have felt unwell if you had left me. So I felt unwell in advance, just so you wouldn't leave me.

ANGELA: (*Reproachfully*) So you fooled me.

MONSIEUR LEBORDIN: No, I didn't fool you, Angela. Before you arrived, I thought I was going to die. When you rang the doorbell, I was practically unconscious. But ... now I'm alive Angela, I'm not dreaming, am I? I'm not dying?

ANGELA: Oh, come now, how can you talk such nonsense! Someone as sharp as yourself is always fully conscious. I dare say, excessively conscious. Your truths are far more cruel than you are, Monsieur Lebordin.

MONSIEUR LEBORDIN: (*Jumps up*) So—I'm cruel, am I? You think we are cruel? (*Emphasizing*) We, the average men. We, the not-chosen men. But do you know how cruel it is that there are women as beautiful as you? Do you know what a blood-boiling insurrection you are to all other women? Women like yourself should be burnt at the stake. If a man sees such a woman next to another man, it will kill all ambition in him for life. What do you think, how many men come close to being granted a woman such as yourself? The majority of men never attain the woman of their dreams. They live their lives next to the kind of woman they have not chosen but who has chosen them. The kind of woman for whom the salary their husband deserves is enough, and for whom the man they deserve is enough. Angela, if an ordinary man sets eyes on you, he would willingly give up reproducing altogether, and for at least ten days, wouldn't even be able

Act I

to look at the Vienna schnitzel his wife breadcrumbs.
ANGELA: Be quiet!
MONSIEUR LEBORDIN: Even now I have to be quiet? At the ripe old age of sixty, when, as far as I'm concerned, you might as well be the most beautiful woman in the world. (*Gently*) Have I offended you? Was I rude?
ANGELA: Not your manner but your words. Nevertheless, I think I could learn more from you than from Professor Henri.
MONSIEUR LEBORDIN: You are a very unfaithful employee, mademoiselle Angela. You haven't even taken the job yet, and you've already denounced your boss.
ANGELA: Please, please drop the facade—stop these games—I beg you! Tell me why you live so alone. Even when there's someone with you, you instantly want to chase them away.
MONSIEUR LEBORDIN: I hate pity.
ANGELA: But, Monsieur Lebordin, hate itself is pitiable.
MONSIEUR LEBORDIN: Are you saying this because you are a good person, or you're just trying to be clever.
ANGELA: Monsieur, God be with you! (*She wants to go*)
MONSIEUR LEBORDIN: (*Simply*) If you leave now, I'll die.
ANGELA: (*Moved*) Do you mean it as you said it?
MONSIEUR LEBORDIN: I said it as I meant it!
ANGELA: Where is your family? Your children? Your grandchildren? Where are they? Why are you so alone? Why are you so pitifully alone?
MONSIEUR LEBORDIN: Because they hate me.
ANGELA: And why do they hate you, Monsieur?
MONSIEUR LEBORDIN: Because they think that I love the vases more than I love them.
ANGELA: And do you really love the vases more?
MONSIEUR LEBORDIN: And why shouldn't I? Supposing I loved my children more than the vases, would my vases hate me for that?
ANGELA: I happen to know that today is your sixtieth birthday.
MONSIEUR LEBORDIN: How do you know that?
ANGELA: Because you're mentioned in Meyers Encyclopedia.

Vase of Pompeii

MONSIEUR LEBORDIN: Interesting. That would never have occurred to me.

ANGELA: Where is your family? Why aren't they congratulating you?

MONSIEUR LEBORDIN: You congratulate me, Angela.

ANGELA: I did congratulate you. I brought you sixty red roses, Monsieur Lebordin.

MONSIEUR LEBORDIN: (*Realizing*) And I didn't want to put your flowers in water. Because the Vase of Pompeii is the most beautiful vase I have. As if the figures on it would be scared of a little flood when they have already survived a catastrophe of gargantuan proportions.

ANGELA: Forgive me, but there can be no greater catastrophe than being left so alone at sixty.

MONSIEUR LEBORDIN: The catastrophe is not that I am alone, but that I survived at all. There was a time when I almost died.

ANGELA: What do you mean ...?

MONSIEUR LEBORDIN: I tried to commit suicide (*There is noise from outside*)

ANGELA: Monsieur, is there someone else in this apartment?

MONSIEUR LEBORDIN: Not to my knowledge. (*The noise is heard again*)

ANGELA: Then there must be a thief outside.

MONSIEUR LEBORDIN: Unlikely.

ANGELA: How old were you then?

MONSIEUR LEBORDIN: When?

ANGELA: When you wanted to die. (*The noise is heard again*) Listen, there is someone out there!

MONSIEUR LEBORDIN: Does that bother you? What are you so concerned about? Did you leave something in the hallway?

ANGELA: No, but ...

MONSIEUR LEBORDIN: Well, then. (*Pause*) I was fifteen years old, mademoiselle, and ... I wanted to die because of a woman who was as beautiful you. (*Angela instantly leans forward and wants to know*)

MONSIEUR LEBORDIN: All right, I'll tell you. It so happens that

Act I

I've never told anyone about this. (*The door opens, and a tall boy enters in short pants. He has a book in one hand and is eating an apple with the other*)

ANGELA: You see! I told you there was someone else here! Is this your grandson?

MONSIEUR LEBORDIN: Oh no. My grandchild is a girl.

ANGELA: Then, who's this boy?

MONSIEUR LEBORDIN: That's me, at fifteen.

ANGELA: (*She stares intensely at the boy, her eyes bulge, she jumps up alarmed face to face with the boy, who is so surprised by her reaction that the apple gets stuck ... and he starts to choke*) It's not possible.

MONSIEUR LEBORDIN: (*He watches the scene with great interest*) He'll suffocate in the end. Hit him on the back a few times!

ANGELA: (*Recovering from shock. Goes to the boy and hits him on the back a couple of times*) There, you'll be all right.

ROBBIE: (*Gasping for breath but unhappy*) Thank you very much, mademoiselle Angela.

ANGELA: Good heavens, how do you know my name?

ROBBIE: Really, mademoiselle Angela, that's extremely unkind of you ...

ANGELA: Unkind ...? I don't even know you.

ROBBIE: Mademoiselle Angela, Just because he is here you don't have to pretend you don't know me.

ANGELA: What are you talking about?

MONSIEUR LEBORDIN: Let him be! (*Almost aside sotto voce*) You were curious about a certain episode, and it's too late to back out now, you must play your part! I was fifteen years old. I was desperately in love with an extremely beautiful woman—who had someone else. You were renting a room at our place. You forgot to lock the door. I came in. Robbie came in and found you with your 'friend'. You begin to see the picture, Angela?

ANGELA: But how is it possible that the boy doesn't recognize you?

MONSIEUR LEBORDIN: How could he recognize me? I know what he was like at fifteen, but how could he know what he'll be like at sixty.

ANGELA: (*Nods understandingly and takes over the part of* ANGELA THE KEPT WOMAN) Robbie, be reasonable! You know how fond I am of you.

ROBBIE: (*Very bitterly*) You're fond of me ... fond of me, but in front of your ... 'friend', you don't even know me.

ANGELA/KEPT WOMAN: (*In a hushed tone*) Robbie, for God's sake, keep your voice down!

ROBBIE: (*Shouting*) I won't keep my voice down. On the contrary, I'm glad that I've finally met up with him! With Mr. Moneybags here!

ANGELA/KEPT WOMAN: Robbie, keep quiet! He is a world-famous art collector.

ROBBIE: I couldn't care less. I am not the least bit interested. All I see is a vile spider weaving his web around you.

ANGELA/KEPT WOMAN: How many times have I told you that there's nothing going on.

ROBBIE: How many times have I told you that I don't believe it!

ANGELA/KEPT WOMAN: But it's true!

ROBBIE: (*Civilized protest*) Then why does he come here all the time? What does he want from you? I know why you send me on errands. But the other day I spied on you, I know everything ...

ANGELA/KEPT WOMAN: (*Unguarded*) If you talk to me like this, if this is how little you trust me, then we will never see each other again!

ROBBIE: Yes, you're always threatening to move out. Well, I'm not threatening, Angela. If you move away, Angela, I'll kill myself.

ANGELA/KEPT WOMAN: How can you speak such madness. Think of your mother!

ROBBIE: You think of my mother!

MONSIEUR LEBORDIN/ART COLLECTOR: (*A delicate reminder*) Mademoiselle Angela, can you see how much I love you?

ROBBIE: It's not true, he doesn't love you, he's just buying you. Because he knows that I'm poor and have only my life to give.

MONSIEUR LEBORDIN/ART COLLECTOR: (*Roughly*) Shut your mouth already, you snotty kid! You bore me!

Act I

ROBBIE: What did you call me? (*With a flushed face, and he picks up the Vase of Pompeii*)
ANGELA/KEPT WOMAN: (*Shouts at him*) Put it down! Put it down immediately! Robbie, put it down! (*Robbie puts the vase down*) Now leave us. Please, leave us for just for a moment! I want to talk to Monsieur Le Directeur!
ROBBIE: (*Capitulating*) All right, I'll go. Because I want you to know how much I trust you.
ANGELA/KEPT WOMAN: You see, this is the way I like you. Like a little boy. Shouting, and jealousy. Every man knows how to be rude.
MONSIEUR LEBORDIN/ART COLLECTOR: I trust this wasn't meant for me, dear Angela (*He stands up*) Stay where you are young man. I'm the one who's going. I'll wait outside. I am sure there is no need to clarify anything, mademoiselle? Between the two of us everything is quite clear. (*With a superior gesture he exits into the hallway*)
ROBBIE: (*Turns after him*) Shall I kill him?
ANGELA/KEPT WOMAN: (*Simply*) No, Robbie don't kill him. I need him.
ROBBIE: I can work. I can support you.
ANGELA/KEPT WOMAN: My dear boy, you may be able to support me, but you could never earn enough for me.
ROBBIE: But I could. Believe me, love is capable of miracles.
ANGELA/KEPT WOMAN: Has your mathematics improved?
ROBBIE: No.
ANGELA/KEPT WOMAN: So, when it comes to math problems, even love stops short.
ROBBIE: Mademoiselle Angela, you're mistaken. Love is one thing, and mathematics is another. I adore you, but algebra is hopeless. It's just hopeless.
ANGELA/KEPT WOMAN: Another bad grade.
ROBBIE: (*Shamefacedly*) Two.
ANGELA/KEPT WOMAN: Well, is this the sort of man you are? Is this what you promised me?

ROBBIE: (*Bursts out*) It has nothing to do with manhood! Nothing whatsoever. Do you understand?!
ANGELA/KEPT WOMAN: It is not difficult to be rude, Robbie.
ROBBIE: Angela, Angela, you can ask me for anything, take my life ...
ANGELA/KEPT WOMAN: Robbie, you must stop throwing your life away. Life is a very serious business.
ROBBIE: But what else can I offer you? My life is all I have to give.
ANGELA/KEPT WOMAN: Promise me that your mathematics will improve.
ROBBIE: I promise.
ANGELA/KEPT WOMAN: And promise me that this promise will amount to more than just a promise?
ROBBIE: You insist on torturing me again. It may interest you to know that you're the one who's responsible for my bad grades.
ANGELA/KEPT WOMAN: Me?
ROBBIE: Yes, you. Don't you think I've studied the material, Angela? Don't you realize that I adore you, that all day long I whisper only two things, your name and the discriminant: minus b plus or minus the square root of b squared minus 4 ac over 2 a. Doesn't that tell you how much I love you?
ANGELA/KEPT WOMAN: No mistake with the plus or minus?
ROBBIE: No mistakes, mademoiselle. And if you want me to, I'll quote you Pythagoras' theorem as well.
ANGELA/KEPT WOMAN: Why did you say that you got bad grades because of me?
ROBBIE: That's just how it is. He's been picking on me ever since you came in.
ANGELA/KEPT WOMAN: Who has?
ROBBIE: The math teacher. The last time he gave me a bad grade I was furious and I told him that he was being completely unfair because nobody studies harder than me. "Well then," he said sarcastically, "you'd better send in your private tutor and I'll discuss the matter with her." I think he's giving me these bad grades just so he'll have a reason to talk to you!

Act I

ANGELA/KEPT WOMAN: (*Visibly likes the story*) Then why didn't you tell him that I'm not your private tutor.

ROBBIE: (*Sheepishly*) I couldn't tell him.

ANGELA/KEPT WOMAN: Why not?

ROBBIE: Because if you hadn't gone to see him as my private tutor in January, he definitely would have failed me in the midterms.

ANGELA/KEPT WOMAN: (*Laughing*), So you fell into your own trap. Or maybe you're just jealous of the math teacher as well?

ROBBIE: No, I'm not jealous of him. But by the same token you can understand that I'll never be able to prove my character through math.

ANGELA/KEPT WOMAN: Robbie, you are so touching when you are manly that one day when you become a real man, you will have great success around women with this boyish seriousness.

ROBBIE: Angela ...!

ANGELA/KEPT WOMAN: What is it?!

ROBBIE: Yes it's true, Angela. I love you, Angela.

ANGELA/KEPT WOMAN: I love you too, Robbie. As if you were my very own little man.

ROBBIE: No, not like that, Mademoiselle Angela! Love me in a noble fashion. Let our love be pure as the driven snow.

ANGELA/KEPT WOMAN: But there's no problem with that, Robbie.

ROBBIE: But there is.

ANGELA/KEPT WOMAN: What?

ROBBIE: Not a what ... who. (*He points outside*)

ANGELA/KEPT WOMAN: Now stop it, you must be more respectful.

ROBBIE: Why, why do I always have to be the one who speaks with respect. Why do I always have to be the decent one. Let Monsieur le Directeur be decent for once.

ANGELA/KEPT WOMAN: That's enough, Robbie! To call him indecent, is to call me indecent.

ROBBIE: Tell him to go!

ANGELA/KEPT WOMAN: I'll tell you to go if you continue to talk to me in this manner.

ROBBIE: Angela, I want to talk to you like the heroes talk to the heroines in the tragedies of Racine. My whole life I would speak to you in this way. Only, please, just get rid of the old ...

MONSIEUR LEBORDIN/ART COLLECTOR: (*Enters*) Have you two finished? It is becoming rather boring out in the hallway.

ROBBIE: Angela, please choose, you must choose!

ANGELA/KEPT WOMAN: I have chosen! You'll both be my friends.

ROBBIE: Impossible. You're either mine or his.

ANGELA/KEPT WOMAN: You are mine Robbie, and I am his!

ROBBIE: What, what are you saying? Say it again, I don't understand.

ANGELA/KEPT WOMAN: And I can keep on saying it, and you still won't understand. This is not Pythagoras' theorem. This is higher mathematics. (*In a lighter vein*) And now I'm going to make us afternoon tea. (*Robbie turns away*)

MONSIEUR LEBORDIN: (*Hits himself on the head. Sotto voce to Angela*) I've just remembered that I've left the milk on half an hour ago.

ANGELA: (*Sotto voce*) I think the milk must've put out the flame by now. (*Goes out to the kitchen*)

ROBBIE: (*After an uncomfortable silence*) Sir, may we talk man to man!

MONSIEUR LEBORDIN/ART COLLECTOR: By all means! Sit down.

ROBBIE: Why should I sit down? Must men always talk to each other sitting down?

MONSIEUR LEBORDIN/ART COLLECTOR: Not always, only when they're tired.

ROBBIE: But I am not tired.

MONSIEUR LEBORDIN/ART COLLECTOR: Sit down anyway. Otherwise you might feel like you're are standing in front of your father. And I don't think I'd enjoy that.

ROBBIE: (*Determinedly*) Sir, I have a proposition for you.

Act I

MONSIEUR LEBORDIN/ART COLLECTOR: I'm all ears.

ROBBIE: I'll give you a pint of my own blood!

MONSIEUR LEBORDIN/ART COLLECTOR: God forbid, my blood pressure is already too high!

ROBBIE: Then a pound of flesh. I'll give you my flesh.

MONSIEUR LEBORDIN/ART COLLECTOR: I've been on a strict diet for some fourteen odd years.

ROBBIE: Sir, I'll make a deal with you. I'll be your slave. I'll spend my whole life working for you.

MONSIEUR LEBORDIN/ART COLLECTOR: Now, that's a far more serious offer. And what might you want in exchange?

ROBBIE: Angela, just let me have Angela!

MONSIEUR LEBORDIN/ART COLLECTOR: Why?

ROBBIE: Because I love her.

MONSIEUR LEBORDIN/ART COLLECTOR: Have you ever loved anyone else?

ROBBIE: No.

MONSIEUR LEBORDIN/ART COLLECTOR: Then how do you know that you love her?

ROBBIE: Well ... I mean ... One has to start sometime.

MONSIEUR LEBORDIN/ART COLLECTOR: Yes, one has to start sometime and one must also finish sometime—even with being in love.

ROBBIE: Why is it necessary to finish with being in love?

MONSIEUR LEBORDIN/ART COLLECTOR: Why? All right, pay attention young man! Since you seem to display a leaning for the truth.

ROBBIE: Certainly. I do believe in the absolute truth.

MONSIEUR LEBORDIN/ART COLLECTOR: Then tell me, how many teeth have you got?

ROBBIE: What are you talking about? I've got all my teeth!

MONSIEUR LEBORDIN/ART COLLECTOR: And I barely have any. How fast can you run one hundred meters?

ROBBIE: Fifteen seconds.

MONSIEUR LEBORDIN/ART COLLECTOR: And I only have to

Vase of Pompeii

walk one hundred meters before my heart starts to play up. What do you eat for lunch?

ROBBIE (*As a matter of course*) Whatever is available.

MONSIEUR LEBORDIN/ART COLLECTOR: And I may pick and choose as I please, yet all I'm allowed is milk or at best boiled potatoes, for breakfast, lunch and dinner. Do you understand, my money makes no difference whatsoever. I would give my last franc for just a skerrick of your youth. For me there is nothing else but this girl. My last chance at love. And now even this you want to take from me, when your life, a whole lifetime still awaits you. So many schnitzels and so many loves. Would you rob me of my only remaining pleasure? Would that be a fair thing to do?

ROBBIE: No, it wouldn't be fair. But can the love of an old man for a young woman be fair? What is she supposed to love about you? Your false teeth? An old man like you can only be loved for his money.

MONSIEUR LEBORDIN/ART COLLECTOR: (*Can barely stifle his indignation*) There might be some truth to that, you may have a point. So what are we to glean from a young woman who stays with such an old man? That money means more to her than youth.

ROBBIE: Say that again.

MONSIEUR LEBORDIN/ART COLLECTOR: Have you ever paid for a hat bill? When could you last afford a bottle of Guerlain-Maxime?

ROBBIE: You think that love dies when one spends his last note? That's impossible!

MONSIEUR LEBORDIN/ART COLLECTOR: If it's so impossible, then why has Angela never sent me away? Since you're so young and dashing, and I am so old and revolting.

ROBBIE: What you're saying is ... shocking. It sounds so much like the truth. And because it sounds so much like the truth, it can't possibly be the truth. The truth cannot be this vile.

MONSIEUR LEBORDIN/ART COLLECTOR: Is that so? Well, what do you think, young man? How does she live so well, so apparently unconcerned? Who buys her shoes and clothes? Her un-

Act I

derwear and her stockings? The chocolates and the sweet liqueur that she has no doubt also offered you from time to time. And where does she pay the rent from? Yet your mother needs the money. And Angela is a generous tenant.

ROBBIE: It can't be. (*Buries his face in his hands*) It cannot be true!

MONSIEUR LEBORDIN/ART COLLECTOR: (*Relieved*) Well, that's a little better. At least you're no longer saying that it's not true, only that it cannot be true. But strictly speaking, it is both: true and 'can be true'. It's more than these, it is! Do you admit that I'm right?

ROBBIE: Yes, you're right. You have nothing else but your false teeth and your dirty little truth. I love Angela, and I chose the Angela I believe her to be. She could never be part of your truth, and if she were I would rather give her up lest I should have to give up my dreams.

ANGELA/KEPT WOMAN: (*Comes in with the tray*) Robbie, we are friends, aren't we?

ROBBIE: Yes, Angela, I'll just need a glass of water ...

ANGELA/KEPT WOMAN: Of course ... would you mind. (*Indicating that her hands are full ... Robbie looks at her very seriously and very sadly, then he slowly goes out to the kitchen*)

MONSIEUR LEBORDIN: So? How do you like the boy I was?

ANGELA: Very, very much. He is such a charming presence that I almost chose him a moment ago.

MONSIEUR LEBORDIN: Why wouldn't I believe it, Angela? When I think that such an old lecher stole my first love ... And yet you didn't choose me.

ANGELA: (*In the meantime, she arranges the afternoon tea*) You really were a very lovable boy.

MONSIEUR LEBORDIN: It's hard to accept as you see me now—a tired and broken old man. It is difficult to comprehend how and why sweet and good-looking children turn into such awful adults ...?

ANGELA: (*Curiously*) And after that you never met me again?

MONSIEUR LEBORDIN: On the contrary, you were the only one

I kept on meeting. Always in a different version. Variations on a theme.

ANGELA: (*Gently*) Could you hum this theme to me?

MONSIEUR LEBORDIN: Bend closer Angela. Listen to it. Listen to my heartbeat ...

ANGELA: (*Assuming the role of ANGELA, THE KEPT WOMAN—expecting the worst*) What's that strange smell? Can't you smell it? Where is that boy? Good God, he hasn't tried to pois ...(*She rushes to the kitchen door ... throws it open ... moves back a step*) Dear God ... he's opened the gas! Come, help me! Call the ambulance!

MONSIEUR LEBORDIN: (*Calmly*) Don't worry, Angela. I'm here. Can't you see I survived?!

(Fast Curtain)

ACT II

In the same place, in Lebordin's room. A woman's dressing gown hangs in a cupboard out of sight.

ANGELA: You said something earlier that I still don't get. (*Lightly*) Why don't you drink your milk, Monsieur Lebordin?
MONSIEUR LEBORDIN: I detest milk. I used to drink coffee, with just a dash of milk.
ANGELA: Coffee is bad for your heart.
MONSIEUR LEBORDIN: So is life, but we still go on living. Cards, drinking, horse races, women. We stockpile the excitements. The more damage the better.
ANGELA: Is that the way you lived?
MONSIEUR LEBORDIN: No.
ANGELA: (*Tongue in cheek*) So that's why your heart stayed healthy. It must have been worth it?
MONSIEUR LEBORDIN: On the contrary. I was made ill from never having enough money to live that life. I was sickened by the knowledge that others could drink, play cards, go to the races and womanize.
ANGELA: I don't understand, a clever man, like you ...
MONSIEUR LEBORDIN: Luck doesn't belong to the clever, it belongs to the courageous. Listen Angela! One day we found a dead fish. It was in Bretagne when I was a kid. And we'd been playing at the seashore all day long. It must've weighed at least thirty kilos and was already starting to rot. The three of us could hardly lift it—the skin was so slippery. One of the boys suggested putting the putrid thing onto the rail tracks. I was absolutely horrified, trembling with fear. The fish's skin was so slippery—I was afraid that the wheels of the engine would slide off the tracks and the train might be derailed. That was the moment when my life got derailed. From that moment on, I weighed up everything. And a person who weighs up everything will choose the least

dangerous, the least risky. And whatever contains no risk, is commonplace: the life of the grey ones.
ANGELA: If you saw it all so clearly, why didn't you do something ...?
MONSIEUR LEBORDIN: I did. I never ate fish again.
ANGELA: A rather unfortunate nature I'm afraid.
MONSIEUR LEBORDIN: I know.
ANGELA: You seem to have taken no pleasure in simply being alive. When the mere fact of life itself is happiness. The worst ...
MONSIEUR LEBORDIN: ... is death ... if I may take the words out of your mouth. (*Angela nods*) You know Angela, I always believed that one should die as if, while walking and muttering a poem, one were losing one's glove. This is how easily one should die. In the company of a beautiful woman ... you speak of being happy at long last because she's finally beside you. And then you die ... smoothly. Without bandages. Without doctors. Without going through the process of dying. Without your heirs taking inventory of the inheritance ahead of time. That's how I would like to die Angela ...
ANGELA: Amen.
MONSIEUR LEBORDIN: Why did you say amen?
ANGELA: Because you've uttered life's prayer.
MONSIEUR LEBORDIN: Angela, please love me just a little.
ANGELA: Believe me Monsieur Lebordin, I do love you, just like a father (*Short pause*) But you said something I still don't understand. You said that you believe in feelings and yet you are disillusioned with everything? I don't get it. There is a contradiction in there somewhere.
MONSIEUR LEBORDIN: If you knew the story of my life you'd understand.
ANGELA: Tell it to me.
MONSIEUR LEBORDIN: It's long.
ANGELA: Briefly!
MONSIEUR LEBORDIN: Sixteen thousand francs.
ANGELA: (*Huge pause*) Sixteen thousand francs?
MONSIEUR LEBORDIN: Did you ask me for the brief version?

Act II

ANGELA: Yes, but you have to explain...

MONSIEUR LEBORDIN: You're a curious being Angela. You believe in extraordinary things but one can only talk to you about them as one would talk to a person behind the counter at the chemist. Haven't I forgotten something? Ah yes. Be good enough to give me a box of talcum powder as well. According to you, the only purpose of speech is to make sure that when we ask for matches we get matches and not salted herring. But emotional facts cannot be expressed in words Angela ... if one were nevertheless to attempt it, one would try to speak as one feels, and not worry about whether the other can feel it or not.

ANGELA: Just tell me what happened with the sixteen thousand?

MONSIEUR LEBORDIN: I lost it at cards.

ANGELA: But if you didn't drink...

MONSIEUR LEBORDIN: ... or gamble or go to the races or play cards. But once, I did sit down to play cards.

ANGELA: I see, and you're not a gambler. So people who play cards all their lives and never lose sixteen thousand francs are gamblers. But you, who in one sitting lost that much, you are not a gambler ...?

MONSIEUR LEBORDIN: I didn't gamble for the excitement.

ANGELA: Then why did you?

MONSIEUR LEBORDIN: I needed sixteen thousand francs for someone I was in love with.

ANGELA: Who was she?

MONSIEUR LEBORDIN: You, Angela.

ANGELA: Me?! ... I see, another variation.

MONSIEUR LEBORDIN: (Taps his heart) On the theme.

ANGELA: How did it happen?

MONSIEUR LEBORDIN: I needed eight thousand francs. I had a mere twenty francs of my own and another three thousand that belonged to someone else. I sat down to play with my twenty francs and won six thousand five hundred. But I still needed another fifteen hundred francs. I continued to play and lost the lot. After that I had to keep playing just to win back the three thousand that wasn't mine to lose. I then dropped another thirteen thousand francs. How did it happen? Well, there were people standing around the table. And there was this one chap who said he knew my mother and knew that we owned a piano and got me to sign something several times. Or to be more precise had me sign my mother's name to it for some thirteen thousand francs in total. I felt like the minister of finance with my signature on every banknote.

ANGELA: And afterwards?

MONSIEUR LEBORDIN: Do you realise the implication of forging a promissory note that you will have to make good on. A promissory note on which you forged your own mother's signature. It had to be paid!

ANGELA: And did you pay it back?

MONSIEUR LEBORDIN: Oh, for God's sake, where on earth were we going to find that sort of money? We were poor—we only had two rooms—we had to let one of them to you, surely you remember that?

ANGELA: (*Once again she starts to playact*) Yes, yes, now I remember. And just how did you fix it up?

MONSIEUR LEBORDIN: My mother turned to her brother, whom she had not spoken to in twenty-two years.

ANGELA: Why?

MONSIEUR LEBORDIN: You'll find out. (*The doorbell rings*)

ANGELA: Who is that?

MONSIEUR LEBORDIN/GUSTAVE: I have no idea.

ANGELA: (*Now accepting her new role as the ARTIST'S MODEL*) Won't it be embarrassing for you if they find me here?

MONSIEUR LEBORDIN/GUSTAVE: Not exactly embarrassing, but it might be better if you went into the bathroom. I'll let you know when the coast is clear.

ANGELA/ARTIST'S MODEL: (*Laughing*) Listen to the language.

MONSIEUR LEBORDIN/GUSTAVE: I speak to be understood. (*Angela/Artist's model goes into the bathroom and Lebordin/Gustave goes out into the hallway*) Who is it?

BOB: (*His voice*) Bob.

MONSIEUR LEBORDIN/GUSTAVE: Who?

Act II

BOB: (*His voice*) Bob.
MONSIEUR LEBORDIN/GUSTAVE: Bob who? (*In the meantime, he is opening the door*)
BOB: (*Comes into the room. He is twenty years old, feels awkward and is dressed with impoverished elegance. At first he looks around, then a bit confused he says*) Uncle Gustave, I am Bob, your sister's ...
MONSIEUR LEBORDIN/GUSTAVE: Ya, you're the gambler. Well come in! Lead the way like a lamb to the slaughter.
BOB: Yes, sir, Uncle Gustave.
MONSIEUR LEBORDIN/GUSTAVE: Don't call me uncle. Call me the disgrace of the family. The soulless usurer. A tax collector of the poor. The blood sucker. Isn't that how I'm usually referred to? Well, what are you staring at? Yes, keep staring, it's perfectly true, everything you see has been pawned. They left all this stuff here—pawned. And why not? Or would you have me play the fool? Throw my money away interest-free. Nobody lends cash for free. Doesn't the government collect its due? I am not a charity and I'm not ashamed of my occupation. I give good money for good money.
BOB: I beg your pardon ...
MONSIEUR LEBORDIN/GUSTAVE: Don't beg my anything! You didn't come here to be polite and complimentary to your kindly old Uncle Gustave. And I don't exactly look upon you as a favourite relative either. And why should I? I wonder how your kind of forger would pay up if there weren't usurers such as myself, the disgrace of the family. Except that now we must ask ourselves just who exactly is the disgrace of the family? An honest usurer or a kid who forges promissory notes? They told me you were the best we have. And look what's become of you? A forger of promissory notes!
Your mother also has plans for me to save the hallowed Lebordin name. Ironic don't you think? Me, the man with no name, the one you all disowned should now be expected to save your public reputation. Do you know what your mother said when she stepped in here after twenty-two years? No doubt she was desperate, at her wits end. Do you know what she said? "You've

Vase of Pompeii

hardly changed, Gustave." Yes, Siree, that's all she said after twenty-two years. You see, her pride didn't allow her to say anything else. But she is wrong you know, because I've changed a great deal over all those years. So many honorable people have passed through these doors. Women who wanted to pay the interest with their bodies. Gallant husbands who generously offered their wives in lieu of a bad debt. Honorable people, you understand, who were very happy to borrow money from me when they needed it and very quick to hold me in contempt when they had to pay it back. I lent money, I demanded money in return and I never accepted anything else —that's an honorable human being! So, sit down. You're not getting any present from me either. That I should be the one to save the Lebordin name!
BOB: Please, Uncle Gustave, I'd gladly kill myself if I thought it would help clear things up.
MONSIEUR LEBORDIN/GUSTAVE: This is not a thing. This is forgery!
BOB: Uncle Gustave, you don't understand ...
MONSIEUR LEBORDIN/GUSTAVE: I was at the exhibition this morning. There was a beautiful picture.
BOB: She's very beautiful.
MONSIEUR LEBORDIN/GUSTAVE: It is a beautiful picture of a beautiful girl. But not worth gambling away sixteen thousand francs for. So why did you do it?
BOB: Because I love her desperately.
MONSIEUR LEBORDIN/GUSTAVE: So was there something going on between the two of you?
BOB: Nothing. I swear, Uncle Gustave, nothing! Apart from the fact that I love her desperately...
MONSIEUR LEBORDIN/GUSTAVE: Oh you love her, do you? You probably don't know that only twenty-four hours before your little coup at the card table the picture in question was for sale at a price of three thousand francs. It was raised to eight thousand when they realized they had a sucker. The girl's in cahoots with the painter. He's been painting nudes of her for years. It's an old scam. Just before an exhibition she looks for a pigeon,

Act II

preferably a rich one. She tells him her tale of woe. What a decent girl she is ... how dreadfully ashamed she is ... everyone is going to stare at her naked body, the lechery—the indignation etc. etc. The turkey feels sorry for her and he buys the painting. That's what happened. She pulled a fast one over you with the painter. They've been lovers for years.

BOB: (*Very indignant*) Uncle Gustave, that's impossible!

MONSIEUR LEBORDIN/GUSTAVE: Maybe you'd rather hear it from her mouth?

BOB: I don't believe it. That girl is untouched. Her reputation is impeccable. No one at the academy was held in higher esteem. I never even dared to consider approaching her before that night at the cafe. There she was, her eyes red from crying. I couldn't help myself. She told me that she was sick with guilt. That she had just posed naked for a portrait because ...

MONSIEUR LEBORDIN/GUSTAVE: ... she needs the money to support her elderly parents...

BOB: (*Startled*) How do you know?

MONSIEUR LEBORDIN/GUSTAVE: The fact that you don't is why I'm the usurer and you're the stooge.

BOB: Nobody could've seen that face at that moment and said anything other than: "Yes, I will buy the picture and it shall be yours as a gift from me to you."

MONSIEUR LEBORDIN/GUSTAVE: As a matter of fact, I said nothing and bought the picture anyway. (*From the top of the low cupboard, he takes the picture that is leaning back to front against the wall and he turns it around—it is Angela's nude*)

BOB: (*With an outbreak of joy*) Uncle Gustave, thank you, a thousand times thank you.

MONSIEUR LEBORDIN/GUSTAVE: My dear boy don't thank me! I only paid three thousand for it.

BOB: I better hurry. I must tell her immediately. She'll be overjoyed.

MONSIEUR LEBORDIN/GUSTAVE: I'm afraid, you won't be going anywhere for the time being. You owe sixteen thousand francs that you cannot pay. And if I don't give it to you, the commonly held suspicion that you won't be able to pay will become a sad reality and you will go to jail.

BOB: Uncle Gustave, I will do anything…

MONSIEUR LEBORDIN/GUSTAVE: I don't want anything. I want a guarantee that I'll get my money back if I'm good enough to lend it to you.

BOB: I'll do whatever you want me to.

MONSIEUR LEBORDIN/GUSTAVE: Very well then, grab that pen and write! And this time sign it with your own name, unusual as that may be for you. "To the Right Honorable Monsieur Gustave Couloise …" —Yes, that should be sufficient for a usurer. I have often been referred to that way by many a dignitary who required my services at various moments of crisis. (*Clears his throat*) "I hereby acknowledge that I, Robert, often known as Bob Lebordin, did forge my mother's name, Madame Nicole Sandrine Lebordin, on a promissory note in the amount of sixteen thousand francs …"

BOB: Uncle Gustave, I can't put this down in writing. A confession like this could ruin me.

MONSIEUR LEBORDIN/GUSTAVE: Then don't write if that's how you feel. I don't want to force you and I don't want to give you the money either. Goodbye nephew. Tsk, tsk … A ruined man at your age. One wonders what you could possibly have to be proud of. Let's hope that should we perchance meet again another twenty-two years from now, you will have changed for the better, or at the very least no longer be a scurrilous forger of promissory notes.

BOB: Please, be good enough to continue dictating Uncle Gustave.

MONSIEUR LEBORDIN/GUSTAVE: Yes, now where were we … address, amount of money, oh yes … "I will do everything within my power to repair this wrong. This is a letter of guarantee. I, Robert Lebordin, am now in debt to the Right Honorable Monsieur Gustave Couloise, and I will do everything within my power to repay him the outstanding amount represented by my promissory note. More than that, I will be tireless and ceaseless in my

Act II

effort to repay the sum stated, as quickly as is humanly possible." Signed, Robert Lebordin.

BOB: Just one little thing, Uncle Gustave, I am starting my exams right now.

MONSIEUR LEBORDIN/GUSTAVE: No, in actual fact you already finished your exams. Your mother and I agreed that you'll be leaving your university studies. I have a friend at the prefecture who will employ you as a copier in the registrar's office. You'll report to him tomorrow.

BOB: (*Almost crying*) Uncle Gustave, everyone at university says that I can look forward to an outstanding academic career.

MONSIEUR LEBORDIN/GUSTAVE: All you can look forward to is jail, my boy. Or would you rather save the family honor? It's all the same to me.

BOB: Your last words were ...

MONSIEUR LEBORDIN/GUSTAVE: "'Signed, Robert Lebordin."

BOB: Vile ... vile ... bloodsucking usurer!

MONSIEUR LEBORDIN/GUSTAVE: (*Cheerfully*) Well, it's about time! I was beginning to think this might be difficult. (*He puts a promissory note in front of Bob*)

BOB: What's this?

MONSIEUR LEBORDIN/GUSTAVE: A promissory note. It is not the first time you've signed one.

BOB: (*Looking at it in disbelief*) But twenty thousand.

MONSIEUR LEBORDIN/GUSTAVE: Oh, come come, did you think I'd give you the sixteen thousand out of love? (*Bob signs it without a word*) Let's see it. (*Lebordin holds up the promissory note against the light*) You've got a nice scrawl. They'll make good use of it in the registrar's office. Now would you like to have a word with her.

BOB: With whom?

MONSIEUR LEBORDIN/GUSTAVE: With your model.

BOB: Angela is here?

MONSIEUR LEBORDIN/GUSTAVE: And why not. Finer than her have graced this room, I can assure you. (*Towards the bath-*

room) Angela, you may come out now. (*Angela/Artist's model comes out of the bathroom*)

BOB: Angela, what are you doing here?!

ANGELA/ARTIST'S MODEL: (*In a vulgar voice*) Spare me the surprise, please. If you'd bought the picture, we'd be at your place now. He bought it ...

BOB: (*Bitterly*) And you with it?

ANGELA/ARTIST'S MODEL: Dear me, embittered cardsharp. Anyway, it's none of your business.

MONSIEUR LEBORDIN/GUSTAVE: That's not fair, Angela, he is not a cardsharp. He is the pride of the family. Soon to be a mere scribe, but the pride of the family nevertheless, and his modified cursive's a joy to behold.

BOB: He was right. You're not worth it.

ANGELA/ARTIST'S MODEL: (*To Lebordin*) He is insulting a lady! Say something!

MONSIEUR LEBORDIN/GUSTAVE: (*Sarcastically*) You're a clever girl, Angela. You can stick up for yourself.

BOB: She's clever, but she's no girl.

ANGELA/ARTIST'S MODEL: How dare you say that to me?! Gambler!

MONSIEUR LEBORDIN/GUSTAVE: Tsk, tsk, not a gambler—forger.

BOB: Thank you for your generosity, Uncle Gustave, I won't forget it. (*He rushes out*)

MONSIEUR LEBORDIN/GUSTAVE: I saved the family honor!

ANGELA: It must have been terrible for you, monsieur.

MONSIEUR LEBORDIN: Those next ten years were truly terrible. I worked day and night to pay back every single one of those twenty thousand francs. And as I struggled to repay those last few francs, Uncle Gustave was already dying. In his final days, he converted everything into cash. Jewelry, government bonds, the lot. And with his dying breath, he took that almighty wad of cash and threw it into the fire. This was his final gesture to the family. I was his sole beneficiary. He left me this picture. Your picture, Angela.

Act II

ANGELA: Honestly, Monsieur Lebordin, turn it around please.
MONSIEUR LEBORDIN: Why so ashamed? Because you're naked or because of what you did?
ANGELA: How can you say that? Was it me who did it?
MONSIEUR LEBORDIN: No, but it could've been you.
ANGELA: Please don't be offended, but I must say, all in all, you haven't had much luck with the opposite sex.
MONSIEUR LEBORDIN: That may be true —between twenty and thirty I hardly had any time to even look at a woman. And while I was finishing paying out my dear uncle, I also completed the degree that had been denied to me before.
ANGELA: So in the end you did get your degree?
MONSIEUR LEBORDIN: Yes. When I was thirty.
ANGELA: Why didn't you become a professor?
MONSIEUR LEBORDIN: Didn't have the right connections. And then there was the business with the cards. Do not imagine that such a youthful stumble would be forgiven by those who stumble all their lives. Society is never angrier than when someone doesn't want to resemble it. I didn't want to. I wanted to repent for my crime. In a court of law I would not have gotten ten years. I spoke with a lawyer, who told me that because of the extenuating circumstances of this particular case—the passion, the madness of my love for you—I'd be a free man within ten months. You see that's the path I should've taken, instead of doing penance for ten long years. As it is, never having received lawful punishment, I am perhaps even today considered guilty. But the only thing I'm really guilty of is that I did not want to be guilty.
ANGELA: You're a mysterious one, I'll say that for you.
MONSIEUR LEBORDIN: Not really. You're the reason for everything. The woman I longed for all my life but could never possess.
ANGELA: Well here I am.
MONSIEUR LEBORDIN: And what does that mean?
ANGELA: I shall be your compensation.
MONSIEUR LEBORDIN: Why, thank you, Angela. You are too,

too kind. And how on earth do you imagine that you could compensate me for the last forty years of my life.
ANGELA: I wish I could, but I can't. I can't change your memories, but perhaps I can ameliorate them. Better to dwell on love unrequited than on disappointment fulfilled ...
MONSIEUR LEBORDIN: Only a woman could say something like that.
ANGELA: And only a man could keep churning over the past. That's why you men smoke pipes, so you'll have something to gnaw on.
MONSIEUR LEBORDIN: Bit by bit, you'll tell me all the love aphorisms of world literature. You don't have to console me, Angela, you don't have to feel sorry for me. I have some very beautiful memories, even in relation to you. They didn't all leave me in the lurch, my Angelas. There was an Angela to whom I only needed to lie ... she didn't even want money.
ANGELA: And why didn't you lie?
MONSIEUR LEBORDIN: I couldn't lie.
ANGELA: But one must absolutely lie to a woman.
MONSIEUR LEBORDIN: No, no, I couldn't lie to myself. That, for me, it didn't matter any more ...
ANGELA: I can't follow your emotional state.
MONSIEUR LEBORDIN: Please, try ... let's continue to play it! You see, one night as I was walking my fiancée home, a streetwalker was coming towards us. You could see she was beautiful or, to put it more precisely, traces of remarkable beauty still lived in her features. As she came closer, too close, my fiancée became alarmed and looked away. Well from that moment on, the streetwalker would not stop following us. Her intention was not to harass, you understand, if anything, she seemed sad and ready to reproach. Arriving with my fiancée at her door, I was given one brief command: "Robert, promise me that you will go straight home." And with that she disappeared through the gate. I barely took a few steps when the streetwalker came right over to me.
ANGELA: (*So far she's been listening intently to every word, and now she takes over the role of ANGIE THE PROSTITUTE. Vulgar accent*)

Act II

Come with me beautiful boy!
MONSIEUR LEBORDIN: I didn't say a word. I continued briskly on my way.
ANGELA/ANGIE THE PROSTITUTE: Didn't Marguerite say anything about me?
MONSIEUR LEBORDIN: How do you know her name?—The question was a complete shock to me.
ANGELA/ANGIE THE PROSTITUTE: Went to school together, didn't we? Oh yes, very proper girl she was, not like me, rotten to the core at an early age. I had an affair with the math teacher because he wanted to fail me, and got myself expelled instead.
MONSIEUR LEBORDIN: I remembered Marguerite's warning. Please, leave me alone. I have no interest whatsoever in your private affairs. Now go away.
ANGELA/ANGIE THE PROSTITUTE: Listen, I don't want anything. I know you're broke. I have known all about you for some time. You're the gambling Lebordin boy. Look, you have to come with me. Up to my house. We'll have a glass of whisky ... because I've just got to talk to someone ... I hope you're religious because I need to own up to something. I know you're a sinner; so am I.
MONSIEUR LEBORDIN: I went, don't ask me why. She told me to go into the bathroom so she could put on a dressing gown.
ANGELA/ANGIE THE PROSTITUTE: (*In a hoarse, common voice*) Well, don't just stand there like a statue. Get going.
MONSIEUR LEBORDIN: (*Staring at her*) Yes, yes, all right. Whatever you say. (*He goes into the bathroom*)
ANGELA/ANGIE THE PROSTITUTE: (*She puts on the dressing-gown and calls out*) You can come out now, I'm ready. (*The thirty-year old Lebordin, who is balding, comes out of the bathroom*) What's wrong, what are you so scared about?
ROBERT: I am not scared. Look here, mademoiselle ...
ANGELA/ANGIE THE PROSTITUTE: Angie. That's what I answer to. No mademoiselle here.
ROBERT: What's your real name?
ANGELA/ANGIE THE PROSTITUTE: Angela. But only my godmother calls me that, so stick to Angie.

ROBERT: Very well, Angie it is. And now tell me, do you make all your clients wait in the bathroom while you change into your dressing-gown?

ANGELA/ANGIE THE PROSTITUTE: None of your business, gambling boy. Why do you want to know anyway? You're not paying, you're not a john. And I want you to treat me like a lady.

ROBERT: So you do want something from me.

ANGELA/ANGIE THE PROSTITUTE: That depends on you, gambling boy.

ROBERT: Robert. That's my real name. And my godmother doesn't call me anything because she's dead. So stop calling me gambling boy.

ANGELA/ANGIE THE PROSTITUTE: But everyone calls you that. That's you, the gambling Lebordin boy ...

ROBERT: So now you're an authority on community politics.

ANGELA/ANGIE THE PROSTITUTE: I've got lots and lots of customers around here.

ROBERT: I'll tell you what, if you give me a drink right now without another word, then I may even become a regular myself.

ANGELA/ANGIE THE PROSTITUTE: (*She takes out the bottle of whisky and the two glasses from the cupboard*) And your fiancée? (*Pouring his drink*) The daughter of Monsieur Latour, Director of the Prefecture? (*She hands him the glass*)

ROBERT: (*With some ceremony, he downs the whole draught, then bangs his glass on the table and takes a deep breath*) I'm still recovering from the worst ten years of my life, Angie. And I don't plan to spend another ten years getting over it. You don't get this sort of conversation every day. This reminds me of university...

ANGELA/ANGIE THE PROSTITUTE: (*She pours him another drink and lifts her glass*) Yes, and that other bitch. (*They drink*)

ROBERT: What bitch?

ANGELA/ANGIE THE PROSTITUTE: The one who got ten years out of you.

ROBERT: Let's not bring that up ... that was a diff...

ANGELA/ANGIE THE PROSTITUTE: Why was it different?

ROBERT: Because I loved her, and to this day I still love her.

Act II

ANGELA/ANGIE THE PROSTITUTE: She must have been some lay, better than me, no doubt?

ROBERT: I can't answer that because I haven't been with either of you. Thank you for inquiring.

ANGELA/ANGIE THE PROSTITUTE: Was she more beautiful than me?

ROBERT: Younger perhaps.

ANGELA/ANGIE THE PROSTITUTE: Yes, so were you. (*She lifts her glass and they drink*)

ROBERT: I know I'm going bald, you don't have to remind me.

ANGELA/ANGIE THE PROSTITUTE: You look exhausted, never mind the hair.

ROBERT: Do you know why I look so tired?

ANGELA/ANGIE THE PROSTITUTE: Why?

ROBERT: Because I am very, very tired. If I slept for another thirty years, I'd still be tired. I'll never recover from this fatigue.

ANGELA/ANGIE THE PROSTITUTE: And now you're going to marry Marguerite? She's so boring.

ROBERT: I'm about to be appointed, Angela. I will be deputy director, with all the privileges and advantages. And quite honestly, I don't really care who I marry if I can't have the woman I love.

ANGELA/ANGIE THE PROSTITUTE: She was a bitch. (*Finishes her drink and pours some more*)

ROBERT: Angela, I'm sure she too had a godmother some time in the past, who did not refer to her as the bitch.

ANGELA/ANGIE THE PROSTITUTE: All right, gambling boy. Don't get upset. Let's have a toast to first names. I want to be on a first name basis with you, especially you. (*They drink and kiss each other lightly*)

ROBERT: Why?

ANGELA/ANGIE THE PROSTITUTE: (*A little drunk*) So that I could tell you what an idiot you are! A woman like that, an absolute slu ... (*Deliberately silences herself with her hand to her mouth*) Oops, better leave work references out of it! Pour it down old chum, drink up boyo. You're the one who's paying for it. What's it to be; daily, weekly or a monthly service.

ROBERT: (*His eyes half shut, he is very relaxed*) Actually, I was rather hoping for a free rental, old chum!

ANGELA/ANGIE THE PROSTITUTE: (*Sobering up*) Maybe, if you play your cards right.

ROBERT: Aha, and what does that mean?

ANGELA/ANGIE THE PROSTITUTE: It means that I am alone. Look at me, Robert. I am as alone as only a woman who deals with many, many men can be. Stay with me Robert, love me ...

ROBERT: Angela, Angela ... maybe as a friend.

ANGELA/ANGIE THE PROSTITUTE: Don't love me that way, Robert!

ROBERT: I could never think of you any other way, Angela. If I close my eyes I can see all those other men standing here in their underpants.

ANGELA/ANGIE THE PROSTITUTE: (*A little hurt*) You're drunk.

ROBERT: (*Shuts his eyes*) No, but it's not a bad idea, it might make them go away.

ANGELA/ANGIE THE PROSTITUTE: (*Drunkenly*) Stop it. I want to talk to you, and I want you to talk to me. Stay with me! Please, I'm asking you, I'm begging you! I've been watching you for a long time, and I like you, I like you a lot. I know your story. I know that you're tired. Stay with me, and you'll never have to do a thing, nor work ever again. As long as you don't beat me! I can't stand being beaten. It's the one thing I could never get used to. Treat me decent, and I'll work in the rain, the snow, anywhere, anytime, all day, every day. Look, I've already made three hundred francs today. We can save it, or you can lose it at cards, it's up to you. You can play cards all day if you like, and I'll just keep working. But there's just one small thing. Only me. No one else. I'm the best there is, so you're not missing anything anyway. I'm a great cook. I can press a man's suit like a tailor. I'll even shave you every day.

ROBERT: I only shave every other day.

ANGELA/ANGIE THE PROSTITUTE: Because it's expensive. But if you no longer have to pay for women or food, or a barber ...

ROBERT: Can you also cut hair?

Act II

ANGELA/ANGIE THE PROSTITUTE: (*Taken aback*) Well—no, but ...

ROBERT: That's a shame, because if you could cut hair, we could've applied for a barber's permit and you could trade in your whore's licence. (*He stands up*)

ANGELA/ANGIE THE PROSTITUTE: Where are you going?

ROBERT: I'm going home, Angie.

ANGELA/ANGIE THE PROSTITUTE: But why are you leaving now?

ROBERT: As Bobby boy, the gambling Lebordin, it's all been rather sweet and silly. But the moment you started calling me Robert, you turned my stomach. Marguerite may have no idea about love, but if it comes down to a choice between her underwear or the image of a long line of strange men in theirs—I'll take Marguerite's underwear.

ANGELA/ANGIE THE PROSTITUTE: Is that so? You think you can just hold me up for a whole hour, and now you want to go without leaving any dough. You must think I make my living out of love.

ROBERT: Will twenty francs do it? And I want a receipt for the drinks. (*Leans on the table*) What is it you really want from me, Angela?

ANGELA/ANGIE THE PROSTITUTE: (*She grabs pencil and paper from the desk*) I want a signed statement from you. It can even be a forgery. I want you to put it in writing that life has some meaning.

ROBERT: It has, Angela.

ANGELA/ANGIE THE PROSTITUTE: (*In tears*) Get out, get out, leave me alone.

ROBERT: Angie, go to the country, become a housekeeper. Learn to cut hair—do something, just get out of Paris. Stop this disgusting work and never do it again. Don't you realize how beautiful a woman is when she gives herself for love alone. And do you know how terrible it is when she does it for anything else.

ANGELA/ANGIE THE PROSTITUTE: Look who's talking!?

Vase of Pompeii

You're selling yourself so you can inherit the position of the Director of the Institute of Antiquities.
ROBERT: That's not why, but to be able to teach people the difference between a Corinthian vase and a Cretan one.
ANGELA/ANGIE THE PROSTITUTE: Lebordin, you're insane. You don't mind if I take back the first name business? Mad Monsieur Lebordin sounds more natural. Would you really—for a vase ...?
ROBERT: Not for a vase. For all the vases in the world. Do you realize how many vases there are still buried under the ground?
ANGELA/ANGIE THE PROSTITUTE: What kind of vases are we talking about? Glass vases? One of my customers is a glass wholesaler ...
ROBERT: (*Laughs*) I think we'd better just leave it there. Suffice it to say that the vases mean to me what getting out of Paris would mean to you: an escape, from the life we lead.
ANGELA/ANGIE THE PROSTITUTE: Do you really think that I could start all over again?
ROBERT: (*Gently*) No. But you could start in the middle. You start in the middle, and when you meet someone who's interested, you tell him the beginning. And if he is still wants to stay with you, you finish the thing together.
ANGELA/ANGIE THE PROSTITUTE: I'm thirty-two years old.
ROBERT: Marguerite is thirty-two, and we're only just beginning.
ANGELA/ANGIE THE PROSTITUTE: Yes, but she's still a virgin.
ROBERT: That only makes it harder for her, Angela. She can never catch up to all the women who started earlier.
ANGELA/ANGIE THE PROSTITUTE: I'd gladly give up that advantage now.
ROBERT: This is a truly bizarre situation. I probably should marry you, but that would be the end of me. I'm so tired I'd simply become a bludger living off your hard work. You see, Marguerite's strength is that she is a dreary, boring woman, who will force me to escape. Marguerite will inspire me into deeper research in the history of art.

Act II

ANGELA/ANGIE THE PROSTITUTE: What should I do? Please, tell me.

ROBERT: You know that joke about virgins. Just keep those thighs together, Angie. No matter how hungry you get, just keep them together. Be strong, be stubborn, press them together. And through your tears go tell those gas lamps on the Boulevard Hausmann, "The shop is closed, bankrupt. I've finished with it. I swear it. I'm going to find a new life. I have to find a different occupation."

ANGELA/ANGIE THE PROSTITUTE: And what possible good will come of that?

ROBERT: Angie, listen to me! This is crucial. You are a wonderful constant temptation for me. Even more so because you are so much better than your profession. If you stay here, I won't be able to live without you. I don't want to live with you! And I don't ever want to lead a life of the mundane. I want something, no, I need something to lift me upwards ... Angela, please you must go away, and one day we'll both be grateful.

ANGELA/ANGIE THE PROSTITUTE: You're a strange one, Robert. But I respect you, I respect you as a man, as a real man. And if my life does manage to change ... you'll be in my thoughts until the day I die. But I want to remember you with a clean-shaven face! So go and put some soap on. (*Robert goes into the bathroom*)

MONSIEUR LEBORDIN: (*Comes out of the bathroom*) So she shaved me and we said goodbye to each other. In my whole life I could never have imagined a more beautiful goodbye. We couldn't embrace because she had a bowl of shaving cream in one hand and a razor in the other. So I gave her a kiss on the forehead and left. I heard nothing from her for six years, until I received my doctorate in art history. But it seems that she followed the events around me, and she suddenly appeared to congratulate me in person. I always felt that I can thank her a little for my doctorate. She was fat and as sparklingly clean as the air in Switzerland. She had her two adorable little sons with her. Twins no less, and what do you think her husband did for a living?

Vase of Pompeii

ANGELA: He was a barber.

MONSIEUR LEBORDIN: No, he was a butcher and sausage maker. He was an enormous hunk of a man. Marguerite refused to receive them, and she went out, which only made it more pleasant for the three of us. We dined on delicious cold meats, hand-cured by the good butcher. We danced, we laughed, we sang funny, bawdy songs and Angie was determined to get undressed to prove that she wasn't so fat after all. And even though Maurice was fully aware of everything, and I mean everything, about his wife's past, his only regret was that she still couldn't cut hair. Maurice was as bald as a cue ball, by the way. As they were leaving, we had a toast to the future, and swore that if I should have a daughter—Marguerite was expecting—they would be the godparents, and therefore, as her godmother, Angie would name my daughter Angela. Marguerite did not return until the next morning. Actually, my father-in-law came in before she did and inquired of me, in his most pontifical manner, whether I was at all aware of the significance of last night's orgy; and that it might be best, having had a chat with his loving daughter, Marguerite, my wife, as he reminded me, that there was a vacant bachelor studio on the second floor of the house, and it would be best if I were to take my vases up there, and receive my guests up there from now on. The joint apartment, on the other hand, should and would be maintained for proper, clean family life. I was taken aback as I realized that this boring duo had inadvertently granted me my most secret desire—to be up there, away from them—up there with my vases. Marguerite then announced that there was a witness to the passionate lovemaking that had occurred between Angie and myself while her husband snored dead-drunk on the couch right next to us. And that since I had made love to Angie, marital relations between Marguerite and myself would cease from that moment on. Thus ended our second and final quarrel. The first had occurred when my son was born and I had wanted to give him my own name. Marguerite and her father had decided early on that my dear Uncle Gustave was the only redeeming light in a rather questionable resume, and together insisted that our son should be called Gustave. Her father, Monsieur le Directeur of the Institute of Antiquities, was in particular very insistent. The position that I had to have. The position that I couldn't afford to jeopardize. The position that I needed for my work! When our little girl was born they christened her Marguerite after her mother. And so I love my vases even more.

ANGELA: No, I can't understand it. The children were still your children.

MONSIEUR LEBORDIN: Yes, there can be no doubt about that. But it was Marguerite who raised them.

ANGELA: And why didn't you raise them?

MONSIEUR LEBORDIN: Partly, because she didn't allow it. And in any case, I didn't have the time.

ANGELA: So it's thanks to your selfishness that your children were estranged from you.

MONSIEUR LEBORDIN: It's possible. I have a passive nature. I like comfortable solutions.

ANGELA: You're not much of a fighter, are you.

MONSIEUR LEBORDIN: One requires peace as an academic. Research demands it.

ANGELA: Hiding behind a sentence again. Your whole life was like that so far. To stand aside from the problems, not to shoulder the fight, to hide under a safe cover.

MONSIEUR LEBORDIN: It's not true, Angela!

ANGELA: But it is. You're no tragic hero, you're not a victim of fate, you always just waited for the manna to fall into your lap. Believe me, in many ways your Uncle Gustave was far more striking than you. You see, he acquired whatever was meaningful in life to him: power over women and men and power over money.

MONSIEUR LEBORDIN: So you too would've chosen him?

ANGELA: I would've chosen the one who is convinced of his own truth.

MONSIEUR LEBORDIN: How could I have had my truth when I was a forger of promissory notes!

ANGELA: Then go to jail or become a pimp, but don't pay with your whole life for the error of one moment. You constantly chose to be a slave of your fate and not its master. There's nothing more tedious than a man offering excuses for how unmanly he was all his life.

MONSIEUR LEBORDIN: You have no right to pass judgement. You don't yet know the last chapter.

ANGELA: Whatever it is, it can't possibly be exciting enough to keep me here any longer. (*She is getting ready to go*)

MONSIEUR LEBORDIN: Angela, please, don't go! When you want to go, I always feel that I'll die, that you're taking my life with you. If you don't know the last chapter, you can't give the final verdict.

ANGELA: What, then? What is it?

MONSIEUR LEBORDIN: A refutation! A refutation of all that you just said about me. Yes, at the age of forty I did put the fish onto the train tracks. The train smashed it and just kept on going. That is the truth. Stay there, Angela! I'll bring in the photo of Lebordin at forty. I posed for it when I was elected deputy director and won the title of Doyen at the Sorbonne. It was a beautiful year. For the first time in my life, I felt that I was a man. That I knew a lot, a great deal. And then, at a meeting of the Sorbonne archaeological society I met an American girl ... (*he goes out*)

ANGELA: (*Immediately transformed, becomes ANGELA THE AMERICAN MILLIONAIRESS*) Strictly speaking it's not entirely proper that I came up to your apartment, Robert. (*The balding, forty-year-old Monsieur Robert, crawls out from under the desk*)

MONSIEUR ROBERT: A lady may visit a museum from time to time, even if it is in a man's apartment. That blasted rubber is nowhere to be found.

ANGELA/AMERICAN MILLIONAIRESS: What will your family say about this?

MONSIEUR ROBERT: You think they'll reproach me for losing my rubber?

Act II

ANGELA/ AMERICAN MILLIONAIRESS: You know what I'm talking about.
MONSIEUR ROBERT: Well, what will your family say about it?
ANGELA/AMERICAN MILLIONAIRESS: Which particular aspect?
MONSIEUR ROBERT: The having seduced a married man with two children aspect.
ANGELA/AMERICAN MILLIONAIRESS: Robert, believe me, I feel deeply ashamed about this.
MONSIEUR ROBERT: Perhaps if something had transpired, but we cannot be held accountable for simple thoughts alone. (*He caresses her cheek, and she enjoys it*)
ANGELA/AMERICAN MILLIONAIRESS: I mean, it's not as though we're clandestine lovers.
MONSIEUR ROBERT: Not even that.
ANGELA/AMERICAN MILLIONAIRESS: When you get your divorce I'll become your wife. And I shall be a virgin, because I saved myself for you, Robert.
MONSIEUR ROBERT: Yes, it seems to be my lot in life to marry virgins.
ANGELA/AMERICAN MILLIONAIRESS: And does that bother you?
MONSIEUR ROBERT: No, no, not at all. It's not virginity that bothers me. It's that if I want to possess a virgin, I have to marry her.
ANGELA/AMERICAN MILLIONAIRESS: You're in a strange mood. Are you angry about something?
MONSIEUR ROBERT: It's not your fault. Tell me ... don't you think I'm too old for you? (*A little pause*) I'm forty.
ANGELA/AMERICAN MILLIONAIRESS: Forty? I thought you were at least ten thousand years old.
MONSIEUR ROBERT: Nine thousand, nine hundred and ninety-nine maybe.
ANGELA/AMERICAN MILLIONAIRESS: You are the first man, and I am the only woman. That's all that counts.

Vase of Pompeii

MONSIEUR ROBERT: All right, let's see it (*He gets involved in the game. He picks up the Vase of Pompeii*) You are going to the creek for water. That's when I spot you. On your shoulder is a pitcher—not just any pitcher—a rare Neolithic pitcher, of which there are only two in the whole wide world. One is in the British Museum (*he directs the vase to her shoulder*), and the other is on your shoulder as you walk gracefully by the river. (*Angela walks with the vase on her shoulder*)

ANGELA/AMERICAN MILLIONAIRESS: Are you watching me or are you watching the pitcher?

MONSIEUR ROBERT: Angela, your shoulders are absolutely gorgeous but the pitcher ... the pitcher!

ANGELA/AMERICAN MILLIONAIRESS: You'd rather have the pitcher than the girl. (*Angela puts the vase back on the coffee table*)

MONSIEUR ROBERT: Don't be upset darling, I love you very, very much.

ANGELA/AMERICAN MILLIONAIRESS: As one loves a reliable assistant.

MONSIEUR ROBERT: No, no. I love you as only a forty-year-old man can love a twenty-year-old girl—decidedly, dependably and irrevocably.

ANGELA/AMERICAN MILLIONAIRESS: I don't like 'dependable' when it comes to love. It sounds to proficient.

MONSIEUR ROBERT: Well, shouldn't a forty-year-old man be proficient on the subject of love?

ANGELA/AMERICAN MILLIONAIRESS: You're doing it again. Don't talk about love in that way. Physical love is not the only kind of love in the world. There's such a thing as a meeting of minds.

MONSIEUR ROBERT: Do you know what a meeting of minds is? When a man thinks about cream cheese pancakes all day long, all day he craves nothing else but cream cheese pancakes, and when he goes home desperate for the taste, lo and behold, someone has prepared cream cheese pancakes for him—that's a meeting of minds.

Act II

ANGELA/AMERICAN MILLIONAIRESS: You're rather cynical aren't you?

MONSIEUR ROBERT: Let's just say I have no more illusions, and when I say that I love you, it is as solid and tangible and real as the finest mathematical equation.

ANGELA/AMERICAN MILLIONAIRESS: I'll wager you were a wonderful mathematician.

MONSIEUR ROBERT: Funnily enough, no. But even today, I still feel this unshakeable respect for its exactitude. Minus b plus or minus the square root of b squared minus 4 ac, over 2a. (*He is thinking*) I can't seem to recall Pythagoras' theorem.

ANGELA/AMERICAN MILLIONAIRESS: Would you like me to tell you?

MONSIEUR ROBERT: That won't be necessary. Let's not emphasise the age difference any more than we have to. Angela, do you know that, compared to you, I am a veritable pauper. A modest little bureaucratic civil servant ...

ANGELA/AMERICAN MILLIONAIRESS: My father's millions disturb you?

MONSIEUR ROBERT: Not your father's millions, but the fact that you are his sole heir.

ANGELA/AMERICAN MILLIONAIRESS: Is it so terrible to be rich?

MONSIEUR ROBERT: Of course it's not terrible. But I've detested the rich ever since I was twenty years old.

ANGELA/AMERICAN MILLIONAIRESS: Are you a socialist?

MONSIEUR ROBERT: Yes, I am.

ANGELA/AMERICAN MILLIONAIRESS: And now you are going to be rich.

MONSIEUR ROBERT: Look, I don't like my family, I never have. It's a terrible thing to say, but that's how it is. I don't like them and have never liked them for many, many reasons that I'm not prepared to go into at this moment. But I will say that the one thing I never disliked about them was their wealth, or rather their lack of it. And now, you see, I'm going to marry you, and I'm going to be rich, and you keep harping on it. And I'm afraid

Vase of Pompeii

that when we are married I may be tempted to think that the only reason I dislike them is because they are poor and that I love you only because you're rich.

ANGELA/AMERICAN MILLIONAIRESS: What are you doing? Are you trying to talk me out of it?

MONSIEUR ROBERT: No, but we have to talk about the not-so-good as well as the good. I have to discuss with you any doubts I may have. I mean, it's not so simple to divorce a woman and two children after ten years of marriage.

ANGELA/AMERICAN MILLIONAIRESS: Tell me honestly Robert, is it they who'll be missing you, or is it the other way around?

MONSIEUR ROBERT: This isn't a question of anybody missing anyone. We are proposing a formal divorce with all its consequences. This is a very serious issue. When it comes down to it, these last few years haven't been a bed of roses for Marguerite either. Nevertheless I have to do the right thing. One dishonorable choice, and all is lost. I simply won't know myself after that.

ANGELA/AMERICAN MILLIONAIRESS: Robert, stop torturing yourself. You won't be shortchanging them. On the contrary, you'd be a bad father, irrespective of the fact that you no longer want to be with them, if you miss this opportunity to truly improve their lot.

MONSIEUR ROBERT: Then I'd be a bad father, but at least I'd still be a father!

ANGELA/AMERICAN MILLIONAIRESS: Robert, I love you so much. I love you so very much. When I read Vases without Flowers, your first book, I felt that it had to be you and no one else. Whatever it cost you, there was so much wisdom in that book.

MONSIEUR ROBERT: Oh, it's wisdom you want. (*Angela nods*) Well, how about this. You only chose me because you have money. Because you could choose me. Had you been a poor girl, for there must be some poor girls somewhere in America, I could never have possibly been an option for you. You would've had to work for your daily bread. You'd have never had the free time to even take an interest in archaeology and consequently you'd

Act II

never have gained an invitation to a meeting of the Sorbonne Archaeological Society.

ANGELA/AMERICAN MILLIONAIRESS: That may all well be very true, Robert, but what does it matter when we're here now, and I love you. I love you desperately, Robert. (*She runs over to Robert, they embrace and kiss passionately. The sound of the doorbell is heard*)

MONSIEUR ROBERT: Angela, would you be embarrassed now if someone discovered you here with me?

ANGELA/AMERICAN MILLIONAIRESS: Embarrassed? So embarrassed that I would happily hang a plaque around my neck, proclaiming that I'm yours and yours alone, for the whole world to see. (*Monsieur Robert goes to the door and returns quickly*)

VOICE OF LATOUR: (*Offstage*) Robert open this door immediately.

MONSIEUR ROBERT: (*In a loud whisper*) It's my father-in-law. Please be patient, he's very stubborn. Prepare yourself. (*He hurries back to the door. He's opening the door*)

MONSIEUR ROBERT: Monsieur le Directeur.

LATOUR: Well you certainly took your time, Robert. I hope I'm not interrupting anything. (*Latour strides into the room*) Good evening!

ANGELA/AMERICAN MILLIONAIRESS: Good evening!

MONSIEUR ROBERT: Papa, please allow me to introduce Mademoiselle Angela Malcolm. Angela, this is Monsieur le Directeur Latour.

LATOUR: (*In a loud nasal voice*) Is this her?

MONSIEUR ROBERT: Yes, papa.

LATOUR: Mademoiselle, I have a bad opinion of young ladies who frequent the apartments of men, and I have a bad opinion of Americans per se. You appear to represent both, so there is no need for me to express my opinion of you.

ANGELA/AMERICAN MILLIONAIRESS: Robert, please ...

MONSIEUR ROBERT: Angela, my dear, would you please wait out on the balcony for a moment, while Monsieur Latour honors me with his visit.

Vase of Pompeii

ANGELA/AMERICAN MILLIONAIRESS: I have no reason to feel ashamed, and as an American through and through, I now find it unnecessary to tell you what I think of you as a European.

MONSIEUR ROBERT: Exactly what I was planning to convey to Monsieur le Directeur.

ANGELA/AMERICAN MILLIONAIRESS: I think my fiancée should best deal with this. (*Takes in Latour for a moment, then exits to the balcony*)

LATOUR: Robert, I received your letter and while reading it I was careful to bear in mind (a) that you are my daughter's husband and (b) that you are of weak character.

MONSIEUR ROBERT: Papa, please ...

LATOUR: Monsieur le Directeur to you.

MONSIEUR ROBERT: As you wish Papa. Very well then, Monsieur le Directeur.

LATOUR: Before you elaborate on your letter, I want to remind you that, although I am no longer your active superior, I can still cause you a great deal of harm at the Institute.

MONSIEUR ROBERT: Monsieur le Directeur, under the circumstances your tone is inappropriate. With all due respect, you have no idea who this lady is—the lady I'm going to marry. She is the daughter of one David Malcolm, whose bank, the Wisconsin Prudential, recently financed a loan to France, in excess of two hundred million dollars.

LATOUR: (*Surprised*) I see you've made up your mind.

MONSIEUR ROBERT: Monsieur le Directeur, please understand me! For the last four years I have not had marital relations with Marguerite. Naturally, over such a long period of time one would have thoughts of other women. I am a man after all. I have no doubt that you and Marguerite were aware of this state of affairs. The purpose of my letter is to inform you that this tacit understanding will now be resolved in a formal separation. I wish to be honest and make an open stand and consequently avoid any dishonor over my decision to either myself, or my fiancée.

LATOUR: Have you thought about your children?

MONSIEUR ROBERT: I've accounted for the children in my

plans, and I can assure you, Monsieur le Directeur, that I shall be able to provide much more for them as a wealthy man in the future.

LATOUR: Have you gone quite mad? Do you really believe for one moment that my daughter, Marguerite, would accept even one filthy centime of your sordid generosity? The second-hand charity of some woman, and I hesitate to call her that, who has openly shamed her and humiliated her. If that's what you believe, then you really don't understand us at all, and obviously never could have, which was my own regrettable mistake in the first place. What on earth was I thinking, that after such a shocking stumble, with us as an example to aspire to, you might have pulled yourself together. And now the only solace left to me, one with which we Latours endure the greatest calamities—is dignity. Dignity when faced with blackguards beneath our class. (*Latour turns his back on Robert and slowly exits the room. Robert stands paralyzed*)

ANGELA/AMERICAN MILLIONAIRESS: (*Comes in from the balcony*) I have just understood the French Revolution.

MONSIEUR ROBERT: Yes, unquestionably there is a dignity in these people.

ANGELA/AMERICAN MILLIONAIRESS: And nothing else except for a fond recollection of the days of yore when they could still whip their serfs to death. Tell me, just what are they so proud of? Is it those prerogatives that gave them the right to shove others into rightlessness?

MONSIEUR ROBERT: (*With some pique*) Angela, your father is a proud man isn't he?

ANGELA/AMERICAN MILLIONAIRESS: Yes, but that's different.

MONSIEUR ROBERT: What is he so proud of?

ANGELA/AMERICAN MILLIONAIRESS: He is justifiably proud of having made his own fortune.

MONSIEUR ROBERT: Well, these people are proud of not having made their own fortune; which, by the way, no longer exists, thanks to the French Revolution.

Vase of Pompeii

ANGELA/AMERICAN MILLIONAIRESS: Are we having a fight?
MONSIEUR ROBERT: You're absolutely right. It's over. Anyway, at least now I won't have to deal with Marguerite any more.
ANGELA/AMERICAN MILLIONAIRESS: In a way it's a shame, because I was hoping to meet your children.
MONSIEUR ROBERT: Never mind, Angela! The children are not our problem any more.
ANGELA/AMERICAN MILLIONAIRESS: Does she love you?
MONSIEUR ROBERT: Yes.
ANGELA/AMERICAN MILLIONAIRESS: How did she endure it for four long years?
MONSIEUR ROBERT: Dignity. They have dignity. They are willing to submit themselves to the most awful suffering so no one will think they are suffering.
ANGELA/AMERICAN MILLIONAIRESS: What a strange woman. Is she beautiful?
MONSIEUR ROBERT: Angela! She was my wife. I can't just talk about her as if she was a piece of furniture.
ANGELA/AMERICAN MILLIONAIRESS: Please, forgive me ... (*in a different voice*) I brought the vase.
MONSIEUR ROBERT: (*As if struck by lightening*) And you mention it just like that? Where is it?
ANGELA/AMERICAN MILLIONAIRESS: It's in my bag out in the corridor.
MONSIEUR ROBERT: You've left it in the corridor?
ANGELA/AMERICAN MILLIONAIRESS: Don't worry. No one has taken it, I'll go and get it. (*But she doesn't move*)
MONSIEUR ROBERT: What is it Angela? What's got into you?
ANGELA/AMERICAN MILLIONAIRESS: Robert, I'd like so much for you to like it.
MONSIEUR ROBERT: What kind of talk is that? If it's as you described it and an original ... Don't be angry. I'm so excited. I'll bring it in (*He starts to go*)
ANGELA/AMERICAN MILLIONAIRESS: One minute, Robert. I would just like to add that America's foremost scholars have argued for half a year about whether it's an original? I would like

it, I would like it so very much for it to be an original. It depends on you alone. In such matters you are considered the foremost authority in the world.
MONSIEUR ROBERT: (*Shocked, laughing*) Angela, if it's an original then it's an original. Now, do you want to get it? You wanted to bring it in, didn't you?
ANGELA/AMERICAN MILLIONAIRESS: (*With a very fine movement she caresses the hand of Monsieur Robert*) You are so good. (*She goes out. Monsieur Robert drums with his fingers impatiently on the desk*) Angela comes back. She carries the vase as if it were a child in her arms. In reality there's nothing in her arms. Very carefully, she hands it to Robert. It is our dearest child. (*Monsieur Robert takes it from her as if it were really a vase. He takes it towards the light. He turns it round and round, puts it on the corner of the desk, takes a few steps backwards*)
MONSIEUR ROBERT: (*Then, in a confident voice*) In this case the father is completely certain. It is Mark Pellion's, the Spanish sculptor's deceptively good reproduction, from 1873.
ANGELA/AMERICAN MILLIONAIRESS: Impossible!
MONSIEUR ROBERT: You said that in this area I am the foremost authority in the world.
ANGELA/AMERICAN MILLIONAIRESS: Impossible that you wouldn't consider it an original.
MONSIEUR ROBERT: But that's how it is. If you want, I swear upon everything that's sacre ...
ANGELA/AMERICAN MILLIONAIRESS: (*Distraught, she holds her head in her hands*) Upon our love?
MONSIEUR ROBERT: Yes.
ANGELA/AMERICAN MILLIONAIRESS: Don't. For the sake of our love ... look at it again. It cannot be a reproduction.
MONSIEUR ROBERT: But it is. If ten seconds is not enough to establish it, then I am not an expert.
ANGELA/AMERICAN MILLIONAIRESS: Okay, so let's say it's a reproduction. Then I'm asking you, I'm asking you for the sake of our love to say that it's an original ...
MONSIEUR ROBERT: I cannot say that.

ANGELA/AMERICAN MILLIONAIRESS: And if I tell you that our happiness, our love depends on it?
MONSIEUR ROBERT: Wait a minute. (*Picks up the phone*) Hello Henri! Good evening it's Robert Lebordin speaking. I'm ringing you to confirm for the record that I've just been asked for an assessment of a vase —supposedly an original from Pompeii. It is in fact, a reproduction. Mark Pellion 1873. Yes ... duly noted? That's all the news. Thank you goodbye.
ANGELA/AMERICAN MILLIONAIRESS: (*Dumbfounded*) What have you done, Robert?!
MONSIEUR ROBERT: I declared my professional opinion without delay, lest love should blind me to the truth.
ANGELA/AMERICAN MILLIONAIRESS: Then we're finished. Do you know that Robert?
MONSIEUR ROBERT: Why Angela? Love is one thing and professional integrity is another.
ANGELA/AMERICAN MILLIONAIRESS: That might be so. But if a man cannot make a sacrifice for his love, then, as far as I'm concerned, he's not a man ...
MONSIEUR ROBERT: For a man the sacrifice is only possible in the reverse—to sacrifice even his love for the truth.
ANGELA/AMERICAN MILLIONAIRESS: (*In complete despair she shouts*) You fool! You miserable old fool! (Runs out of the room)
MONSIEUR ROBERT: (*Runs after her, shouting*) Angela, Angela, the vase! Your vase ... (*The stage stays empty for a moment, then Monsieur Lebordin comes back with Angela. Very tiredly he sits down into an armchair*)
MONSIEUR LEBORDIN: Well, that's how it happened. All I had to do was to reach out, and I simply threw her away. I threw her away in the name of truth.
ANGELA: (*Points to the vase in which her roses sit*) Is this the vase?
MONSIEUR LEBORDIN: It is.
ANGELA: You appear to hold it in high regard for a forgery.
MONSIEUR LEBORDIN: (*Very broken, very tired*) I T I S N O T A F O R G E R Y!
ANGELA: Whaaat?

Act II

MONSIEUR LEBORDIN: Not a forgery! Six years later, I realized without a shadow of a doubt that it is an original. This vase was in Pompeii and saw the eruption of Vesuvius.
ANGELA: Then you really are a fool.
MONSIEUR LEBORDIN: As are all men who are prepared to sacrifice their love for the alleged truth. Later I wrote a book and dedicated to Angela Malcolm. It was called Vase of Pompeii. I wrote asking for instructions about what she wanted me to do with the vase. She wrote back thanking me for the dedication and said that I should keep the vase as it was responsible for all her happiness ... She has a gorgeous two-year-old son and a husband whom she adores and who adores her. If their time allowed it, they would visit me one day. Her husband is very grateful to me ... And holds my academic work in high regard ...

(Slow Curtain)

ACT III

When the curtain rises, Angela is standing with her back to the audience. She uses an old-fashioned camera to take a picture of Monsieur Lebordin who is sitting in the right armchair. Fifteen-year-old Robbie is lying at his feet. On the right and left arms of the chair sit the thirty-year-old Robert and the forty-year-old Monsieur Robert. Behind the armchair stands twenty-year-old Bob with his arms folded. Full lighting as Angela is about to take the picture. The lighting narrows gradually until only Lebordin is fully lit.

ANGELA: All right. Hold still. I want to capture you just as you are, one, two three! All done. (*Angela moves but all the other characters remain rigidly in their respective poses*) Well what is it? Finished. Don't you underst...

MONSIEUR LEBORDIN: (*As if coming out of a reverie*) Oh yes, finished. Thank you Angela. I'm now immortalized on the occasion of my sixtieth birthday.

ANGELA: And what about the others? Don't you understand? It's finished. You can all go.

MONSIEUR LEBORDIN: (*A little irritated*) Who can all go? What are you talking about? There's only the two of us here.

ANGELA: Don't be silly Monsieur Lebordin. I've just photographed them with you.

MONSIEUR LEBORDIN: Photographed who?

ANGELA: The fifteen, twenty, thirty and forty year-old Lebordin.

MONSIEUR LEBORDIN: Angela, how can you say such things? A human being is indivisible.

ANGELA: But when you told me your story, they actually came to life.

MONSIEUR LEBORDIN: But that's all in the past. And the past can be recalled, it can even be re-enacted. But a human being is indivisible just as time is. One cannot say that at twenty-three hours fifty-nine minutes and fifty-nine seconds on the 31st of December in 1492, it was still the Middle Ages, but that two sec-

onds later it was the beginning of Early Modern Times. Furthermore, one can only define something when it has passed. And once it has passed, at best, we can learn from it. Angela, I went through the story of my life with you in chronological order. But as long as I'm conscious nothing can break up this chronological order. Nothing. It is indivisible because it's in the past—it's gone. And it is not possible to return to what's gone. Hence, the tragic connection between man and time. Man is born, develops and then regresses. He disappears without a trace. We try to break up the time into hours, minutes and seconds, so that we may anchor ourselves somewhere. We try to cling to a wall of nothing, which itself is nothing. But only very few know, Angela, that time is indivisible. In vain do we try to hook the hands of the clock between the spokes of its wheels. Time is indivisible, as is the human being.
ANGELA: A human being is divisible. He disintegrates.
MONSIEUR LEBORDIN: Only his corpse. But his memories and his experiences remain, that is what creates the illusion that we are alive—whoever has no memories or experiences hasn't lived.
ANGELA: Then why are you so surprised that the others are here?
MONSIEUR LEBORDIN: They're not here. Because so long as I'm conscious, my experiences can't break through this chronological order. They can't all be here together.
ANGELA: But they are here. They've been here for ten minutes. Once you sat down, they all wandered in here to be photographed with you.
MONSIEUR LEBORDIN: That's not true. I can't see anyone. You're trying to drive me mad. (*Rushes over to the camera and pulls out the plate holder*) No plate. I knew it. I knew that it would be empty. You tricked me. Angela, you tricked me again.
ANGELA: Robert, I swear there was a plate in there before.
MONSIEUR LEBORDIN: Then where is it? You need a plate to photograph a person who's alive.
ANGELA: For a person who is alive, yes. (*Whispering mysteriously*) Your memories, which your body held together like a picture

frame, are in the process of disintegration, Robert Lebordin. (*The lighting narrows even further around Lebordin, who stands in front of the stage*)

ROBBIE: (*A light upon Robbie who, with an apple and a book in his hands, stops before Lebordin*) Do you remember how I nearly killed myself. How that old scoundrel tricked me. And I was so stupid ... if I had taken her in my arms and covered her with kisses, like the flowers cover the cherry trees in May, perhaps our love too would have blossomed that way. But I wanted to speak to her like the hero talks to the heroine in the dramas of Racine, when I should have spoken to her as one speaks to a barmaid. (*Mumbling*) Minus b plus or minus the square root of b squared minus $4ac$ over $2a$. (*Slowly recedes into the darkness*)

MONSIEUR LEBORDIN: (*Falling back into his armchair*) Angela, help him! Don't let him go away so humiliated.

ANGELA: I also cannot alter the past, Robert.

ROBERT: (*A light upon Robert*) Here I am. Angie has a granddaughter now. They christened her Marguerite in honour of your dead wife. They knew each other at school. Angie was already a bad girl then. God be with you, grandpa Lebordin. (*Recedes into the darkness*)

ANGELA: (*Screams out*) Careful, don't knock the vase!

MONSIEUR ROBERT: (*A light up on Monsieur Robert*) Which vase? Oh yea, the Vase of Pompeii. That has an interesting story to it. It was brought to me by an American girl. She was so beautiful. And she absolutely wanted to marry me. Then she didn't marry me. (*Mumbles*) Because the vase wasn't an original. Although it was an original. Almost inconceivable ... (*Slowly recedes*)

MONSIEUR LEBORDIN: Why have they all come to say goodbye? Do you know Angela?

ANGELA: (*A little apprehensively*) Bob hasn't come yet.

BOB: It's you I have to say goodbye to, Mademoiselle Angela.

ANGELA: Me? What do you want from me?

BOB: I want to give you something.

ANGELA: (*Interested*) What is it? (*With all his might Bob pushes his fist into Angela's face and then disappears*)

Act III

ANGELA: (*Screams out*) He hit me.

MONSIEUR LEBORDIN: Impossible. He didn't do it then. The past can't be altered. I don't know how he could do it now.

ANGELA: (*Sniveling as after crying*) Well, he did.

MONSIEUR LEBORDIN: Then forgive him. He's my saddest memory. Let me kiss your hand.

ANGELA: (*Very seriously*) Kiss my face, where he hit me.

MONSIEUR LEBORDIN: (*He leans forward to try and kiss her but can't reach her face. He recoils in horror*) Angela you haven't got a face. I was kissing air. (*Shouting at the top of his voice*) Who are you Angela?

ANGELA: (*Very calmly*) Just a girl.

MONSIEUR LEBORDIN: It might mean success for you, but it's bankruptcy for me. I want you surname Angela!

ANGELA: I haven't got a surname, my dear, I haven't got a surname.

MONSIEUR LEBORDIN: Why 'my dear'?

ANGELA: Because I pity you, Robert Lebordin. God knows how much I pity you. You were not born an ordinary man, yet you led an ordinary life ...

MONSIEUR LEBORDIN: Why, why are you talking about me in the past tense?

ANGELA: Because your life should be an example for others. For other men. It should come out in a book or be serialized in the newspaper.

MONSIEUR LEBORDIN: Finally, I know who you are! You came from the newspaper. You ferreted out all my secrets and now you want to write about them.

ANGELA: You were the one who told me everything.

MONSIEUR LEBORDIN: Because you tricked me. But you won't take my secrets out of here. You'll never get out of here alive.

ANGELA: Robert, please don't threaten. It's beneath us.

MONSIEUR LEBORDIN: Even now playing the unattainable woman. Yet you are exceedingly attainable for those who can give you something. An apple, monthly allowance or some jewelry. I know you. I know who you are.

ANGELA: (*Calmly, coolly*) You don't know me, and you don't know who I am. But you're right about one thing, one of us will not get out of here alive.

MONSIEUR LEBORDIN: Angela, understand me. In my whole life I've never talked to journalists. I've always been a very private person. I never wanted my affairs to be made public. I guarded my secrets in the depths of my heart.

ANGELA: Silly. Do you think you're the only one with secrets? The hearts of the majority of people are riddled with such suffering. The real sensations are not the ones you read on the front page of newspapers. The real dramas are not where the blood flows. The real dramas take place in one's innermost and there's no help. No first aid. Drop by drop, blood trickles out of our hearts, like water from a cracked vase. Have you any idea how much suffering I've seen? If I could make a single violin string out of the sadness that lives in people, on that one string alone I could play humanity's anthem of grief, to which, perhaps even God would pay attention.

MONSIEUR LEBORDIN: (*Sighing*) Angela, you won't ever leave me, will you?

ANGELA: I will leave you, Lebordin, and you will leave us too. You will even leave yourself.

MONSIEUR LEBORDIN: And what will become of the Vase of Pompeii? Will it also disappear with me?

ANGELA: It won't disappear with you, just for you.

MONSIEUR LEBORDIN: Tell me, why must we decompose under the ground and not the buried vases?

ANGELA: Because art is eternal and indivisible. A yearning towards perfection. The only negotiable path towards God.

MONSIEUR LEBORDIN: I don't want to die, Angela. Help me!

ANGELA: I can neither help you live nor die.

MONSIEUR LEBORDIN: I don't want to perish, Angela!

ANGELA: You won't perish; you'll be the fragrance of the flower that grows on your grave. And you'll continue in your children. In them you will live on.

MONSIEUR LEBORDIN: I don't want to live on! I want to live!

Act III

ANGELA: What is it that makes you want to live ...
MONSIEUR LEBORDIN: I want to start all over again.
ANGELA: Ridiculous.
MONSIEUR LEBORDIN: What's ridiculous about that?
ANGELA: That ever since there've been humans on earth, when their last hour strikes, they want to start it all over again. Aren't there enough examples before you?
MONSIEUR LEBORDIN: That's the tragedy of humankind. Every person's life is a physiological experiment whose objective is to put happiness on a firm footing. And so far everyone has perished in this experiment. That's why we want to start all over again. Because based on the lessons of our own life, we think we hold a sure recipe in our hands.
ANGELA: Do you have a will?
MONSIEUR LEBORDIN: I don't. I don't have anything else but the Vase of Pompeii. For me, it was a recipe for unhappiness.
(*Short pause*)
ANGELA: Have you said goodbye to your wife?
MONSIEUR LEBORDIN: Marguerite was angry with me till the very end. I wasn't even allowed to go to her deathbed. She couldn't forgive me for having loved me even on her deathbed. It happens Angela. In fact, it's usually like that. We tend to desperately love the one for whom it doesn't even matter when we die.
ANGELA: (*Quietly, calmly*) Monsieur Lebordin, have you seen the afternoon papers?
MONSIEUR LEBORDIN: (*Whimpering*) No. Is there something of special interest?
ANGELA: Yes. The lilac trees in Normandy have started to bloom ...
MONSIEUR LEBORDIN: (*Whimpers and collapses into an arm chair. He holds his hand to his heart*) Angela ... my heart, it hurts so, Angela ...
ANGELA: Monsieur, Monsieur Lebordin, stay calm.
MONSIEUR LEBORDIN: (*With a death rattle*) Who are ... you ... Angela!

Vase of Pompeii

ANGELA: (*Nestles up to his feet and leans her head onto Lebordin*) I am not a journalist Monsieur ...

MONSIEUR LEBORDIN: (*A very great calm spreads over him, he quietly says*) I always wanted to die this way—while walking ...

ANGELA: I am not a journalist Monsieur Lebordin. And I didn't come here to pry into your secrets. I came to improve your memories and to ease your death. I am the Angel of Death ... (*A light shudder runs through Lebordin and his head tips to one side. Angela rises and takes a few light steps towards the door. The door opens by itself bathing her in a powerful light. She lifts up her hand, holding it as if she were leading someone into a dance with her fingers. She stops at the door and calls out*) Monsieur ... Monsieur Lebordin. Can we go ...?

(Curtain)

THE END

TRANSLATOR'S AFTERWORD

Lajos Walder's secondary education included the study of French and English literature and culture, which were particularly popular with intellectuals in interwar Hungary, while the general public gravitated toward German culture. The Paris depicted in *Vase of Pompeii*, however, should not be read as a mere screen for 1930s Budapest; it equally dramatizes the state of the French bourgeoisie at the time. Given that so much of the play incorporates the author's personal experiences as well as reigning social conditions, moreover, a few comments on historical and biographical context are in order:

Catholicism was Hungary's official religion. Consequently, all Catholic holy days were public holidays. 'Name days' were perhaps even more important than birthdays. Children were mostly named after a saint (usually one whose attributes the parents hoped their child would emulate). Hence, one's name day occurred on a particular saint's day. Each district of Budapest was named after a saint. The given saint's day was celebrated with a procession and a mass, as well as an open-air fête. The less calculating would typically choose their children's godparents from the family circle, or from among their friends. The more ambitious' quest consisted in recruiting godparents from among the wealthy and influential—say, a politician or a financier and his wife. Such a move, if successful, would determine the child's life path.

The Walder family's financial hardships were such that immediately after my grandfather's death, his clothes had to be taken to the pawn shop in order to provide money for food and rent. Six months later, the clothes were redeemed. In Hungary at the time, all pawn shops were government-owned, and the interest rate was regulated by the state. Each suburb had two or three pawn shops, and my uncle Imre, the youngest of the Walder children, recalled that it was his job to physically take things to the pawn shop, because owing to his endearing and affable appearance he would always get a bit more money than his older sisters and brothers. Needless to say, every cent mattered. Private money lenders, such as the play's Gustave, were not in short supply, but the interest they charged would have been prohibitively high—which is why a poor middle-class family like the Walders could never have afforded to approach a private lender. Indeed, the play's twenty-year-old Bob Lebordin can only do so thanks to family connections. (Incidentally, in those poverty-stricken times, owning a piano implied a certain level of financial stability; hence, the man who lends Bob money at the card table thinks him better off than he actually is).

Another source of income for the Walders consisted in subletting two rooms in their four-room apartment, a practice that continued even after the family's financial circumstances had improved somewhat. Eventually, my widowed, ingenious and hard-working grandmother was able to support the family by running a summer rental in "Balaton Lelle"—one of the villages on Lake Balaton (the most popular resort in Hungary)—where she offered modest room and board for the season. In the beginning, there were only a handful of guests. But as the years went by, the business grew and became so successful that just prior to the advent, in the late 1930s, of the Jewish laws in Hungary, which made it illegal for Jews to own property, my grandmother was managing her own hotel: The *Fogas*, or *Perch*, as it was called, catered to one hundred and fifty guests, was renowned for its excellent cuisine, and a particular favourite with Austrian tourists.

In her seminal 1929 book *A Room of One's Own*, Virginia Woolf writes the following about 'Judith', Shakespeare's imaginary sister: "Chastity had then, it has even now, a religious importance in a woman's life, and has so wrapped itself round with nerves and instincts that to cut it free and bring it to the light of day demands courage of the rarest." The moral standard depicted by Woolf was equally binding in 1930s Hungary. Thus, in a society that put a premium on a woman's virtue and that frowned upon divorce as an infraction of the sanctity of family life, it was not uncommon to find thirty to thirty-two-year-old virgins, such as the play's Marguerite. Yet turning into a spinster by the narrow margin of another two to three years was considered the greatest of catastrophes, and spinsterhood was looked upon with pity and contempt. That's why, when the play's Angela, the play's "visitor," tells Lebordin that she is still a girl, he responds with the question: "Will it be success, or bankruptcy?" As in any rigid society, gender relations were riddled with paradox.

Discreetly kept women, such as the play's Angela who rents a room at Robbie's mother's, were tacitly accepted. Examples were often set by people in high places. For instance, it was well known that the emperor Franz Joseph, when in Budapest, had his mistress stay in a special villa close to the castle in Buda; just as it was common knowledge which famous prima donna was the culture minister's (a Catholic priest's) concubine.

Following the great depression, fringe-dwelling con artists, such as Angela, the play's "model," were not in short supply. They were neither accepted nor were they considered total outcasts. Prostitutes, on the other hand, were severely stigmatized. They required a permit and were under police supervision. Their personal ID contained an indelible red stamp that branded them as prostitutes. Thus, when the play's thirty-year-old Robert tells Angie, the play's "prostitute," to leave Paris, he does so with the knowledge that, in the city, she could never break free from the prostitute's stamp.

Robert Lebordin finally receives his first university degree at the age of thirty. There were no part-time or evening courses at Hungarian universities in the 1930s. On the other hand, university students were not required to attend lectures at all. Examinations were scheduled once a year. If a student felt unprepared for them, or failed them, he could retake them the following year. Many of the poorer students who needed to work obtained their degrees by such slow measures, often amounting to several years.

In an era when the vast majority of youngsters left school at the age of fourteen, only one third of students received a high school baccalaureate, which was considered an excellent level of education. A university B. A., meanwhile, was viewed as a uniquely high achievement. Professorial positions often depended on good political connections rather than merit.

In 1930s Hungary (as elsewhere), the general public viewed America as the land of the rich. Not only were there endless entertaining stories about American millionaires and their excesses, but anyone who emigrated to America also seemed to have done much better financially than their impoverished Hungarian relatives back home. An illiterate peasant who worked in the coal mines of Pennsylvania may have earned a pittance by American standards. But a small part of that pittance, which he sent back to his relatives in Hungary, was of great help.

However, both intelligentsia and aristocracy (be they of modest means, as the play's Latour), had a snobbish, haughty attitude towards Americans, whom they saw as the uncultured and vulgar *nouveau riche*; Europe, meanwhile, remained the true home of civilization.

A delusory romantic pathos had long been part of the Hungarian cultural psyche. It even became a proud source of patriotic identity. Consequently, people flattered themselves with Quixotic poses. Thus, the play's Robbie wishes to talk to the "kept" Angela "like the hero talks to the heroine in the dramas of Racine," and the forty year-old Robert, who really does not hesitate to abandon his children, imagines himself honorable just by sticking to convention. "One dishonorable choice, and all is lost. I simply won't know myself after that."

Concerning Lebordin's age—the play takes place on his sixtieth birthday—it is important to recall that in the mid-twentieth century the average life expectancy in central Europe was between fifty and sixty.

Finally, Lebordin is the quintessential bourgeois. Lajos Walder considered it difficult, if not impossible, to escape from that class. But this does not relieve Lebordin of personal responsibility for making choices. Ethically and philosophically, individual responsibility was the highest priority for the playwright.

Available & forthcoming from UWSP

- *November Rose: A Speech on Death* by Kathrin Stengel
  (2008 Independent Publisher Book Award)
- *November-Rose: Eine Rede über den Tod* by Kathrin Stengel
- *Philosophical Fragments of a Contemporary Life* by Julien David
- *17 Vorurteile, die wir Deutschen gegen Amerika und die Amerikaner haben und die so nicht ganz stimmen können* by Misha Waiman
- *The DNA of Prejudice: On the One and the Many*
  by Michael Eskin (2010 Next Generation Indie Book Award for Social Change)
- *Descartes' Devil: Three Meditations* by Durs Grünbein
- *Fatal Numbers: Why Count on Chance*
  by Hans Magnus Enzensberger
- *The Vocation of Poetry* by Durs Grünbein
  (2011 Independent Publisher Book Award)
- *Mortal Diamond: Poems* by Durs Grünbein
- *Yoga for the Mind: A New Ethic for Thinking and Being & Meridians of Thought* by Michael Eskin & Kathrin Stengel
  (2014 Living Now Book Award)
- *Health Is In Your Hands: Jin Shin Jyutsu – Practicing the Art of Self-Healing (With 51 Flash Cards for the Hands-on Practice of Jin Shin Jyutsu)* by Waltraud Riegger-Krause (2015 Living Now Book Award for Healing Arts)
- *The Wisdom of Parenthood: An Essay* by Michael Eskin
- *A Moment More Sublime: A Novel* by Stephen Grant
  (2015 Independent Publisher Book Award for Contemporary Fiction)
- *High on Low: Harnessing the Power of Unhappiness*
  by Wilhelm Schmid (2015 Living Now Book Award for Personal Growth & 2015 Independent Publisher Book Award for Self-Help)

- *Become a Message: Poems* by Lajos Walder
  (2016 Benjamin Franklin Book Award for Poetry)
- *What We Gain As We Grow Older: On Gelassenheit*
  by Wilhelm Schmid
- *On Dialogic Speech* by L. P. Yakubinsky
- *Passing Time: An Essay on Waiting* by Andrea Köhler
- *In Praise of Weakness* by Alexandre Jollien
- *Vase of Pompeii: A Play* by Lajos Walder
- *Below Zero: A Play* by Lajos Walder
- *Tyrtaeus: A Tragedy* by Lajos Walder
- *The Complete Plays* by Lajos Walder
- *Homo Conscius: A Novel* by Timothy Balding
- *Castile: A Novel* by Stephen Grant
- *Potentially Harmless: A Philosopher's Manhattan*
  by Kathrin Stengel

570